"If you are going to read one book on how to study the Bible, this is it! The art of mining the gold of truth from God's Word has never been so well explained and demonstrated in one volume."

—Earle Craig, pastor,
Grace Fellowship Church,
Costa Mesa, CA

THE LANGUAGE OF GOD

A Commonsense Approach to Understanding and Applying the Bible

RON JULIAN, J. A. CRABTREE, AND DAVID CRABTREE

NAVPRESS

Bringing Truth to Life
P.O. Box 35001, Colorado Springs, Colorado 80935

OUR GUARANTEE TO YOU

We believe so strongly in the message of our books that we are making this quality guarantee to you. If for any reason you are disappointed with the content of this book, return the title page to us with your name and address and we will refund to you the list price of the book. To help us serve you better, please briefly describe why you were disappointed. Mail your refund request to: NavPress, P.O. Box 35002, Colorado Springs, CO 80935.

The Navigators is an international Christian organization. Our mission is to reach, disciple, and equip people to know Christ and to make Him known through successive generations. We envision multitudes of diverse people in the United States and every other nation who have a passionate love for Christ, live a lifestyle of sharing Christ's love, and multiply spiritual laborers among those without Christ.

NavPress is the publishing ministry of The Navigators. NavPress publications help believers learn biblical truth and apply what they learn to their lives and ministries. Our mission is to stimulate spiritual formation among our readers.

ISBN 1-57683-276-7

Cover design by Jennifer Mahalik
Cover image by DigitalVision
Creative Team: Steve Webb, Eric Stanford, Amy Spencer, Pat Miller

Some of the anecdotal illustrations in this book are true to life and are included with the permission of the persons involved. All other illustrations are composites of real situations, and any resemblance to people living or dead is coincidental.

The quotations that begin each chapter are from *Alice in Wonderland* and *Through the Looking-Glass and What Alice Found There* by Lewis Carroll.

Unless otherwise identified, all Scripture quotations in this publication are taken from the *New American Standard Bible* (NASB), © The Lockman Foundation 1960, 1962, 1963, 1968, 1971, 1972, 1973, 1975, 1977, 1995. Other versions used include the *Revised Standard Version Bible* (RSV), copyright 1946, 1952, 1971, by the Division of Christian Education of the National Council of the Churches of Christ in the USA, used by permission, all rights reserved; and *The New English Bible* (NEB), © 1961, 1970, The Delegates of the Oxford University Press and The Syndics of the Cambridge University Press.

CIP data applied for

FOR A FREE CATALOG OF
NAVPRESS BOOKS & BIBLE STUDIES,
CALL 1-800-366-7788 (USA)
OR 1-416-499-4615 (CANADA)

Printed in the United States of America

1 2 3 4 5 6 7 8 9 10 / 05 04 03 02 01

To all those who have sacrificially
helped and supported the ministry
of McKenzie Study Center over
the last two decades

Contents

A Call to
Common Sense

IT HAS OFTEN BEEN noted that common sense is not as common as the term would lead us to believe. This has been particularly true in recent decades, it seems. Many have begun to question whether we can know anything about the world with real trustworthiness. That philosophy results in skepticism and despair. Others, to the contrary, argue that our Creator made us to be knowers—that our senses and minds were designed to provide us with reliable information about the world. Theirs is a call to return to common sense. This book is a similar call.

In our time people approach the Bible in a variety of ways. In academic circles the Bible is viewed as a collage of different oral and written sources. In this view, study of the Bible is the exclusive domain of highly trained experts, who are the only ones equipped to deal with it competently and responsibly. Such experts are so focused on their search for different sources within the biblical text that they can see no coherence. Because they are working with a disassembled text, it is not surprising that the results of their academic labors are often meager and sometimes patently nonsensical—hardly something on which to build one's life.

At the other end of the spectrum (if approaches to the Bible could be so arranged) is the perspective that the Bible ought not to be studied but merely meditated upon. In this view, serious study of the Bible is discounted as intellectualizing and runs the risk of missing the simple meaning within it, whereas one can gain immense benefit from merely meditating on the words of the Bible. But because the message that one finds by meditating is not derived from the meaning of the text itself, many different and even contradictory messages could come from the same text. Using this approach, how can one ever proclaim with confidence, "Thus saith the Lord"?

In the view of the authors of this book, both of these perspectives are wrong but both have something right. In order to make good sense of the Bible, it must be the object of serious study, but one need not be a trained expert. God chose to put His message in a form accessible to virtually every human being. If you can talk and think, you can understand the Bible. Good Bible study is basically just the application of common sense to the words of Scripture. God made the Bible to be understandable to man. God made man to be a knower, capable of understanding His revelation. It takes work (a lot of work!), and some are more gifted at it than others, but in principle anyone can learn to interpret the Bible, even if only to learn to distinguish a correct interpretation from an incorrect one. As you will see, the principles of interpretation are not difficult to grasp—you use them every day. However, the application of those principles to some passages of Scripture can be extremely difficult. By appealing to your common sense, this book is an attempt to cut through much of the confusion about how to interpret the Bible. We hope that what we present strikes a chord and that you will gain a renewed confidence in the ability of the Bible to speak meaningfully and authoritatively.

To demonstrate how this approach to interpretation is applied to a passage of Scripture, we have chosen to use James 5:13-20. We hope that our treatment of this passage is a helpful and instructive example. Space did not allow us to include a fully developed commentary on this section of James that would address all of the interpretive issues. However, such a commentary exists on our Web site. If our discussion of the passage raises further questions regarding our interpretation, please consult our Web site: www.mckenziestudycenter.org. Every chapter concludes with a list of study questions. The authors of this book have written their own responses to these questions as a way of expanding upon some of the points of this book at greater length. You can find these answers on our Web site as well. We encourage you first to try to answer these questions yourself and then to look at our Web site to see how we would respond to the same questions.

This book is the product of a team effort. The seminal elements of this perspective were developed by J. A. (Jack) Crabtree during his years as a pastor at Peninsula Bible Church in Palo Alto, California. They were further developed as a result of discussions that have taken place over the past twenty years at McKenzie Study Center, where all three authors work and teach. Although Jack did the trailblazing, it is fair to say that every staff member of McKenzie Study Center has played a role in forging the ideas presented here. The authors share a common perspective on biblical interpretation, but each articulates that perspective differently—this accounts for the differences in style that can be seen from one chapter to the next. In the pages that follow we hope, if not to persuade you of the soundness of our approach, at least to stimulate your thinking about the important topic of biblical interpretation.

CHAPTER ONE

Can We Understand the Bible?

"Let's consider your age to begin with—how old are you?"

"I'm seven and a half exactly."

"You needn't say 'exactually,'" the Queen remarked: "I can believe it without that. Now I'll give *you* something to believe. I'm just one hundred and one, five months and a day."

"I can't believe *that*," said Alice.

"Can't you?" the Queen said in a pitying tone. "Try again: draw a long breath, and shut your eyes."

Alice laughed. "There's no use trying," she said: "one *can't* believe impossible things."

"I daresay you haven't had much practice," said the Queen. "When I was your age, I always did it for half-an-hour a day. Why, sometimes I've believed as many as six impossible things before breakfast."

ONCE UPON A TIME, a weary band traveled through the wilderness on a journey to a great city called Wisdom. The road was straight but very long, and they wondered if they would ever arrive. One day they came upon an old, weather-beaten sign that read, "Turn right to enter into Wisdom." At first the travelers were delighted. This was exactly what they needed—a sign that would show them the way to Wisdom. It had such a simple message, too. Simple . . . and yet, what did it mean? The travelers started to argue among themselves over the meaning of the sign. Soon the travelers had split into factions, each with its own interpretation of the enigmatic sign.

One group said, "The meaning of the sign is obvious. Surely we should interpret it in the most natural and literal way. Although the road goes straight ahead, the sign is telling us to abandon the road and 'turn right.'" And so they left the road and walked off into the wilderness.

Another group stepped forward and said, "The meaning of the sign is obvious. Surely the makers of the sign do not intend us to leave the road; the road is here for a reason. The sign must be telling us to turn sideways and face to the right as we walk down the road. That makes sense, because the door into Wisdom is exceedingly narrow; only those who walk in sideways will fit through the door." And so they all rotated a quarter turn to the right and walked (somewhat clumsily) sideways down the road.

A third group took a turn at explaining the sign. "The meaning of the sign is obvious. Surely the other groups were taking the sign much too literally. Wisdom is not a physical city; it is a way of thinking. If we want to enter into Wisdom, we must abandon our leftist, liberal political views and 'turn right.'" And so they sat down at the side of the road to form a new chapter of the Young Republicans.

Those in the last group, having heard the first three groups, shook their heads sadly. "What use is this sign? Each group is convinced that they understand it, and yet they cannot agree on what it means. This sign is of no value in showing us the way to Wisdom." And so they turned around with heavy hearts and went back the way they came.

The authors of this book believe that the Bible can be understood. And we are not alone. Multitudes of Christians throughout the centuries would join their voices with ours, testifying that the Bible has a clear, understandable message that points the way to salvation. Unfortunately, the value of all this unanimous praise for the Bible's clarity is undermined by one thing: although we all agree that the Bible can be understood, we cannot agree on what it means. We are like those groups reading the sign in the wilderness: we each are convinced that it is understandable, but we each come away with a different message. How understandable is a message that everyone understands differently?

Am I exaggerating the differences among Bible-believing Christians? Are not the disagreements among Christians mostly about relatively trivial doctrines? No, Christians disagree about the most profound and fundamental issues of the faith. Consider, for example, a much-debated verse from the book of James: "What use is it, my brethren, if someone says he has faith but he has no works? Can that faith save him?" (James 2:14). For some Christians, the message of this verse is clear. The mere act of "believing" the gospel will not result in salvation; we must have the kind of faith that results in a changed life. That is, we must have "works." For other Christians, however, the verse clearly says something different. They deny that eternal salvation depends on our works, and so they conclude that James must have meant something different by the word *save*. Sin has tragic consequences in this life, including physical death, and a faith without works cannot save us from reaping those consequences, although such a faith will save us from hell. Each of these groups has come to essentially opposite conclusions: one group says eternal salvation *does* depend on having works; the other group says eternal salvation *does not* depend on having those works. And both groups are appealing to the same verse: James 2:14.

That Christians disagree over such a fundamental issue is discouraging. By any reckoning, James sounded a life-and-death warning, one that he was anxious for his readers to understand. Yet we cannot agree on what he meant. If the Bible cannot speak clearly about its chief topic—salvation—then how can we expect it to speak clearly about anything? The obstacles to understanding seem formidable. Yet the purpose of this chapter, and ultimately the entire book, is to show that the obstacles are not insurmountable.

WHY COMMUNICATION WORKS— AND WHY IT DOES NOT

I HAVE AN urgent message for you: Never step into a crosswalk without first looking both ways. As the author of this important message, I have put my thought into words, and now my work is done. Your work as the reader, however, has just begun. Reading is not a passive process. I am not just pouring my ideas into your head, like pouring water into a basin. My words communicate—if they do—because you know many things already. Think of how many things I have not explained to you because I assume you know them already. To name just a few:

- What is a crosswalk?
- Is stepping into a crosswalk like stepping into a bathtub?
- Why do I say "both" ways? Are there only two ways? Which ways should you look? In front of you and behind you? Up in the sky and down on the ground? Southwest and northeast?
- What is the point of this message? I have given no explanation; why shouldn't you step into a crosswalk without looking both ways?

As the writer, I have assumed that you know that crosswalks are designated spots on roadways where pedestrians walk. You know that "both ways" refers to the two directions on the road from which cars may be coming. You understand that stepping in front of a moving car can kill you, and so you understand why I have given such a warning. As the reader, your mind is actively using your prior knowledge to make sense of my words. Throughout this chapter I am going to refer to this sort of prior knowledge as the reader's *preunderstanding*. Communication works—when it does work—because the author is counting on the preunderstanding of the reader.

Ironically, however, the very preunderstanding that makes communication possible is usually also the culprit when communication does not work. What if I, the author, have assumed the wrong things about your preunderstanding? What if you grew up in a jungle village and have never seen cars, streets, and crosswalks? What if someone reads this book a thousand years from now when all travel is done with Hovercraft and teleportation devices? Communication may break down because there is a gap between the preunderstanding I expect in my readers and the preunderstanding they actually have.

Most English-speaking adults have had enough exposure to Shakespeare to be familiar with the balcony scene from *Romeo and Juliet.* Juliet stands at the balcony, saying, "O Romeo, Romeo! wherefore art thou Romeo?" As a kid, I thought I understood what was happening in this scene (probably because I had watched too many cartoons). Juliet was longing to see Romeo, and she was calling out for him, "Where are you, Romeo? I want to see you." Unfortunately, I had it all wrong. My problem started, I think, because I assumed that *wherefore* was Elizabethan English for "where." But *wherefore* does not mean "where"; it means "why." Juliet is asking, *"Why* are you Romeo?"; that is, "Why do you have the name Romeo, being the son of my family's hated enemy? Why couldn't you have another name and belong to a different family?" All of this I missed because I thought I knew what *wherefore* meant, but I was wrong.

It is easy to see how a gap could develop between my preunderstanding and Shakespeare's. Shakespeare wrote *Romeo and Juliet* around 1595—more than four hundred years ago. Nobody uses the word *wherefore* anymore, although we do use the related word *therefore.* I live in a different world than that in which Shakespeare and his audience lived. It's little wonder that I have to work harder than they did to understand their language.

If such a preunderstanding gap exists when reading Shakespeare, then what shall we say about the Bible? The historical gap between myself and the biblical world is measured not in hundreds but in thousands of years. Shakespeare wrote in a language that I can still recognize as English; the Bible was written in ancient Hebrew, Aramaic, and Greek. I read Shakespeare for entertainment, and usually (not always) I have no strong feelings or stubborn opinions that color how I read him. But the Bible is dealing with some of the touchiest, most personal issues of all. Is there a God? Am I a sinner? What does God think of me? Is my understanding of life all wrong? What do I owe God? What do I owe my neighbor? What is truly valuable? Experience suggests that human beings have strong feelings about these questions, and those feelings are all a part of the preunderstanding we bring to the Bible. Furthermore, many of us come from denominational traditions that have given us a set of lenses through which we see the Bible. We already know what a passage is supposed to mean before we ever actually read it. And so the obstacles to understanding multiply: the Bible was written a long time ago, in a different place, in different languages, with a different view of reality from the world in which we live—a view of reality that we may find personally difficult to accept. The conclusion is inescapable: the preunderstanding gap between myself and the Bible can be huge.

CLOSING THE GAP

WHAT ARE WE going to do? You may have been told in the past that we should come to the Bible with "no presuppositions," that our minds should be "blank slates," that we should just let the Bible "speak for itself." The spirit behind this advice is good. Practically speaking, however, this advice is impossible to follow. When we read, we interpret the words in the light of what we already know. Not only is it impossible for us to stop using our preunderstanding, but also we would not want to stop even if we could. Would we really gain anything if every time we opened the Bible we forgot everything we already knew about God, salvation, and so on? Of course not. We cannot make any sense of what we read without drawing on our prior knowledge.

Yet the problem remains: preunderstanding is essential to communication, but it can lead us astray. When we read words in the Bible like *God* or *salvation,* we already have a preunderstanding of what those words imply, and we may be wrong. Christians have differing ideas about what Paul meant by "faith," and reading Paul's great teaching in Romans and Galatians does not seem to resolve the issue. Every time Paul talked about faith, we all read in our own meaning. How is Paul ever going to get through to us if his meaning is always being swallowed up by the ideas we already have in our heads?

Abandoning our preunderstanding is not going to help us; instead, we want to correct our preunderstanding. We want to close the gap between the knowledge we *do* bring to the text and the knowledge we *should* bring. But is that possible? Many in the modern academic world are saying, "No, it is not possible. Readers are irrevocably locked into their own private world of meanings, and the meaning of the author can never break through." This book is not intended to deal with the ins and outs of this academic debate. I do, however, disagree vigorously with such a skeptical view of communication. Common sense tells us that people can and do change their minds about what a text means. I brought the wrong preunderstanding to *Romeo and Juliet,* but that did not stop me from correcting myself and changing my mind. I have also at times changed my mind about what the Bible is saying. More than once I have argued strongly against a particular interpretation of a passage, only in the end to become convinced of that interpretation and change my mind. This is a normal feature of how people learn.

Furthermore, as Christians, we do not have the option of being skeptical about the possibility of communication. Surely God would not have chosen to communicate in writing if we were incapable of understanding it. Paul told us that the Scriptures are "profitable for teaching, for reproof, for correction, for training in righteousness" (2 Timothy 3:16). That is, people who have the wrong ideas can hear the teaching of Scripture and be corrected. If a faulty preunderstanding doomed us to perpetual confusion, then the Bible could never set us straight. Paul told us that the Bible can set us straight, so it must be possible for language to communicate, even to people whose preunderstanding is wrong.

This book is about how people such as ourselves—people who are ignorant about many things and just plain wrong about many others—can overcome the gap between their faulty preunderstanding and the truth. Let me identify five essential steps to closing that gap:

1. Be willing to change your mind.
2. Gather new information.
3. Follow the author's lead.
4. Imagine all the possibilities.
5. Seek consistency.

I want to talk about each of these steps in more detail.

Step 1: Be Willing to Change Your Mind

The first step is by far the most important: we must be willing to admit that we might be wrong. A mind that is determined to retain its beliefs will do so, no matter where the evidence leads. We all find this easy to understand—when we look at other people. Baptists firmly believe that Methodists and Presbyterians need to admit that they might be wrong. Pentecostals firmly believe that non-Pentecostals should open their minds to other possibilities. What is so easy to see in other people, however, is painfully difficult to see in ourselves. *We* might be the ones in error. *We* might be making wrong assumptions that color how we read the Bible. The journey toward the truth is ultimately a humbling one. To step toward the light means admitting that I have been standing in the dark.

It pains me to say it, but sometimes Christians are the people least open to the possibility that they might be wrong. Those who of all people should understand the need to stand humbly before the truth are sometimes the most dogmatic and arrogant of all. We act as if our conversion were the last time we will ever be called upon to change our minds. This stubbornness certainly shows itself in how we approach the Bible. As a teacher of biblical studies, I often have the opportunity to see Christians debating the meaning of biblical texts. I would like to say that I often see people with different viewpoints actually listening to each other, actually considering the other person's point of view. I would like to say this, but I cannot.

What accounts for the stubbornness with which many Christians approach the Bible? One reason is the naïveté that many have concerning how language works. Many do not understand that they have a preunderstanding or how that preunderstanding can affect what they see in the Bible. People say things like "I do not interpret the Bible; I just read it." In other words, whatever pops into their heads when they read the text is *the* meaning. To such people, any attempt to appeal to the context or to Greek word meanings is just blowing smoke. The meaning of the text is already obvious, and so there is no need to consider any other possibilities. What they fail to see is that the meaning is "obvious" only because of all the prior assumptions they have made. Until we are willing to see that we *always* come to a text with prior assumptions and that those assumptions might be wrong, we will never make any progress in our understanding of the Bible.

Another reason for our stubbornness can be a confusion over what it means to persevere in faith and to stand up for the truth. We rightly recognize that we live in a culture that values "open-mindedness" over truth. In our world it seems as if the only evil is to call someone else wrong. Christians are right to resist the spirit of the age. There is no virtue in such openness. To refuse to believe the truth when it is available to be known is evil. As Christians, we are called to believe the truth and defend it passionately. There is a great difference, however, between believing that the Bible is infallibly true and believing that our own understanding of the Bible is infallibly true. True champions of the truth acknowledge the possibility of their own error. We need not be wishy-washy or unwilling to take a stand. What we must be, however, is willing to follow the evidence where it leads. If others raise valid objections to our ideas, we should be willing to consider their argument and ultimately seek to answer it. If the evidence of the text itself seems to be pulling in another direction, then we should be willing to follow it. If we are right, then our ideas can stand the scrutiny and will vindicate themselves in the end. If we are wrong, then it is better to find out now.

Ultimately, our willingness to reconsider our own thinking is more of a moral and spiritual issue than an intellectual one. Any student of the Bible is called to be a truth seeker. Truth seekers are willing to follow the truth wherever it leads, even if in the process they are proven to have been wrong. This book seeks to help each of us become better listeners so that we can tell when the truth is calling us elsewhere.

Step 2: Gather New Information
Part of our preunderstanding can be researched and checked against objective outside information. Word meanings, grammar, cultural background information—if we are wrong about these things, it is possible to get back on the right road. My understanding of the balcony scene from *Romeo and Juliet* could have been corrected much earlier if I had bothered to look up *wherefore* in a dictionary. Not every interpretive issue

is that simple, but the principle is always the same. In my efforts to understand a text, I need to make sure I am bringing the right information to the text, and many times that information can be checked. A significant part of this book is about learning what kind of information we need to gather, how to gather it, and what to do with the information when we get it.

Step 3: Follow the Author's Lead

Because our minds have a certain stubborn tendency to follow their own train of thought, communication can become a kind of tug of war between the author and the reader. The author's words are trying to pull in one direction, but the reader's mind is pulling hard in another. A stubborn reader can "win" this tug of war, but only at the cost of misunderstanding the text. The careful reader—the one who truly wants to understand the author—will go with the author, paying close attention to how the author has put his words together. The keyword is *context,* and the importance of the context cannot be exaggerated. The context—the particular words the author has chosen in the order he presents them—is the single greatest tool we have for finding an author's meaning.

Context is what we are in danger of ignoring when we proof-text, that is, when we pull a verse out of context and try to prove a point with it. Notice how context plays an important part in understanding the balcony scene from *Romeo and Juliet.* Part of my problem was that I had decided what Juliet meant without reading the whole scene. All I knew was the line "O Romeo, Romeo! wherefore art thou Romeo?" In the context of the scene, understanding her to be saying, "Hey, Romeo, where are you?" makes no sense at all. But *"Why* are you Romeo?" makes perfect sense. She goes on to say, "Deny thy father and refuse thy name. . . . 'Tis but thy name that is my enemy." Everything that follows is about the problem of Romeo's name, that is, the problem of his belonging to a family that has an ancient blood feud with her family. Not only should

I have looked up what *wherefore* meant but also I should have tried to make sense of the entire scene and not just taken one line out of context.

Any author—Shakespeare, a biblical author, anyone—has a coherent set of ideas he is trying to communicate. If we refuse to look for that coherence, then we are setting ourselves up to misunderstand the text. A significant part of this book explores the nature and use of context in the search for the author's coherent meaning.

Step 4: Imagine All the Possibilities

As unlikely as it may seem, suppose that you are wrong in your understanding of a particular passage. What is the journey toward being right going to look like? Maybe at times it will be as easy as looking up a word in a dictionary. Sometimes, however, we will not be prepared to give up our cherished interpretation so easily. That is not necessarily a bad thing. The process of knowing is rightly a conservative one. We do not throw out our deepest beliefs just because a minor problem emerges. We protect our worldview from every little bump in the road with a shock absorber: we give ourselves time to think it over.

Is it possible, however, for us to deal fairly with interpretations other than the one to which we are presently committed? How can we seriously consider an option that we believe to be wrong? Here is where the God-given power of the human imagination comes into play. Before we actually change our minds, we consider the hypothetical possibility that the other perspective is right. We think, *Suppose that were true. What would that mean? How would I interpret this phrase? How would my beliefs have to change?* I do not mean that we are always conscious that we are doing this. But something like this happens whenever we go through the process of changing our minds. We cannot believe six impossible things before breakfast, but we can imagine that we do. We can imagine that we believe what we in fact do not believe, and then we can see where it leads us.

To illustrate what I mean by the use of the imagination, I want to go back to the example of James 2:14 with which we started this chapter: "What use is it, my brethren, if someone says he has faith but he has no works? Can that faith save him?" Let us look at this verse from the perspective of those who argue that eternal salvation is not the issue in this verse.

Their preunderstanding. These interpreters put a lot of emphasis on Paul's teaching on justification by faith (and rightly so). They interpret Paul to have been saying that salvation comes through one simple act of believing, regardless of whether a person repents or perseveres in faith or submits to God in any way. If you have once believed, you are saved. Period. They believe this to be the teaching of the New Testament, and they believe (rightly) that James will be consistent with the rest of the New Testament. Therefore, they approach James 2:14 assuming that James was not connecting eternal salvation with works of any kind.

They are not wrong to make assumptions. If the New Testament truly teaches that salvation has no connection with how we live our lives, then they are right to assume that James would agree. However, the keyword is *if.* Are they in fact bringing the right preunderstanding to James 2:14? I believe that their preunderstanding is quite wrong, but that is a bigger question than we can argue here. (I have explained my own perspective on that question in my book *Righteous Sinners* [NavPress, 1998].) My point is merely that they have a particular preunderstanding and are using it when they read James 2:14.

Their argument. We might legitimately ask these interpreters, "If salvation has nothing to do with works, then why did James say that it does in 2:14?" They would answer that James was not saying that. Their argument would have many facets. One part of their argument deals with James' use of the word *brethren.* They argue that James could not have been talking about salvation unto eternal life because he called his readers "my brethren." If he called them "brethren," that means that he conceived of them as believers who were saved already. Therefore, eternal salvation could not have been what James was talking about; he must have been talking about some other kind of salvation. He must have been saying something like "Faith without works cannot save you from the bad consequences of sin in this life." Faith without works saves us from hell but not from God's discipline.

Now I want to apply our interpretive imaginations to this argument. For the sake of argument, let us imagine a different preunderstanding than the one taken by these interpreters.

Our new, hypothetical preunderstanding. Imagine that James and the New Testament authors did not believe that eternal salvation comes through the mere act of belief. They believed that faith involves a deep change of the human heart. This change necessitates perseverance. That is, a true heart of faith will hold fast to that faith until death. This change of heart also necessitates a change of life. If we genuinely believe the gospel, then we will live as if the gospel were true. Thus faith without "works"—without a visible impact on how we live—cannot lead to eternal salvation, because a true heart-faith must have an impact on how we live. Not everyone who "believes" the gospel has actually made that deep commitment of the heart. Because this is true, James knew that his readers were probably a mixed group. Some of them were mature believers; some of them were immature believers; some of them were "believers" in name only. (Remember, I am not asking those who disagree with this perspective to agree with it; I am only asking them to imagine, for the sake of argument, that it is true.)

Now we come to the crucial question: If, for the sake of argument, we imagine James having the set of beliefs I outlined above, how would he address his readers? Would he refuse to apply an intimate term like *brethren* to a mixed group? Would he say, "You so-called brethren"? Why would we think so? I can easily imagine a pastor standing in front of his con-gregation, knowing that some are true believers and some are not, and saying, "My brethren, we must believe and be saved." Real-life examples are not hard to find. Here is a quotation from an eighteenth-century sermon by Samuel Davies called "The Nature and Necessity of True Repentance": "Now, my brethren, if [a willingness to acknowledge the hidden evils of the heart] be an essential ingredient in true repentance, do not some of you see that you are destitute of it and consequently that you are still impenitent sinners and ready to perish as such?" What is more natural than a pastor graciously using an inclusive word like *brethren* even as he warns his congregation of the eternal consequences of a false faith? Well, the New Testament authors were pastors, and I would expect the same thing from them.

Has this imaginative exercise proven that James *was* talk-ing about eternal salvation? No. We have shown only that the phrase *my brethren* proves nothing one way or the other. Both of the preunderstandings discussed above would fit the use of the word *brethren*. James could have been convinced that every "believer" to whom he wrote was saved, or he could have suspected that some of them were in fact not saved; either way, he might easily have referred to his general readership as "brethren." Those who argue that James could not have been talking about eternal salvation because he called his readers "brethren" have made a poor argument. We have not settled the question of what James meant, but we have made a sig-nificant advance in our thinking about the passage.

If we are willing to consider reasonable alternatives to our current preunderstanding, we can make progress. We are not doomed to repeat our mistakes. One of our goals for this book is to encourage and model this kind of thinking.

Step 5: Seek Consistency

Suppose I were reading the autobiography of an actor well known to be both a liar and a fool. In his book I read, "I graduated from military school at the top of my class because I was an expert on the tactics that General George Washington used to win the Civil War." Now I happen to know that this actor said in an interview that he had dropped out of school. Furthermore, I know that Washington was a general during the Revolutionary War, not the Civil War. My prior knowledge is totally inconsistent with what the actor seems to be saying in his autobiography. How will I, as a reader, respond to the seeming inconsistency?

I may start by trying to resolve it. Was there another George Washington, one who fought in the Civil War? Could the actor have dropped out of school and then returned to graduate at the top of his class? Could "graduate at the top" be slang for "flunk"? Does the dictionary include a definition of *expert* that means "total idiot"? I am not, however, going to pursue this line of thinking very long, if at all. I do not need to find consistency between my prior knowledge and what the actor said, because there probably is none. Is it surprising that a liar and a fool would exaggerate his accomplishments and display his ignorance? I might wish that his claims were consistent with reality, but it does not surprise me to find that they are not.

For a Christian, however, interpreting the Bible is a very different matter. The authors of this book believe in the total inerrancy of the Bible. That is, if the Bible asserts something to be true, then it is true. I recognize that such a statement needs a defense, but this book is not the place to make that defense. We cannot avoid the issue, however, because the inerrancy of the Bible has great implications for the process of interpretation. The Bible speaks the truth, and the truth is always consistent with other truth. If the Bible is true in what it says, then its message is consistent within itself and consistent with the real world. Therefore, we cannot rest with an interpretation that is inconsistent with the rest of the Bible or with reality. We are always seeking a coherent understanding of the Bible and of life; biblical interpretation is a quest for consistency.

At this point the astute reader may be questioning the value of my advice. How can we solve the problem of preunderstanding by "seeking consistency" when in fact the search for consistency confronts us with the problem of preunderstanding in its most acute form? After all, the Bible is inerrant but my understanding of its message is not. If my interpretation of a passage comes into conflict with my preunderstanding of the rest of the Bible, which one do I change? My preunderstanding about the real world is equally subject to error. If my conclusions from the Bible contradict my preunderstanding about life and reality, which do I reject? I have several comments:

1. *Each of these five steps is of value only in conjunction with all the others.* By itself, the process of seeking to reconcile our interpretation with our preunderstanding could easily become a vicious circle. If we start out with a mistaken preunderstanding, we can easily read that into the text we are interpreting, which in turn reinforces our mistaken preunderstanding, and so on. It is only by combining this step with all the others that we can break out of the vicious circle. We must be willing to change our minds; we must gather new and more accurate information about the language and culture out of which the author was writing; we must pay careful attention to the context and seek the author's intention; we must have the integrity to exercise our imaginations and consider other interpretations; and we must seek to reconcile our interpretation with the rest of the Bible and with reality. By doing all these things, we can make genuine progress toward the truth.

2. *The search for consistency is absolutely necessary.* If we cannot reconcile our interpretation of a passage with our understanding of the rest of the Bible or with our worldview, then something is wrong. Yet too many Christians have allowed themselves to amass an incoherent and conflicting set of beliefs about life and the Bible. The search for a consistent and coherent view of life and the Bible is an absolutely necessary part of being a truth seeker. It is not always easy to know just where

we have gone wrong, but knowing *that* we have gone wrong is an important step in itself.

3. The process of knowing is a conservative one. As I commented earlier, we tend to keep our existing preunderstanding until we are compelled to change it. That is the way it should be. When a piece of evidence that seems to contradict our worldview comes our way, we usually refrain from jumping to conclusions. Should I decide that gravity is no longer functioning just because I see a magician levitate his assistant? Should my opinion of God's goodness flop back and forth with every good or bad thing that happens to me? No. Our preunderstanding is—and should be—relatively stable, but it is not immovable. Eventually the evidence can mount against our preunderstanding to the point that we are willing to change it.

For example, I know of many people who started out deeply antagonistic to the idea that God chooses those who are saved, that faith is a gift of God. Over time, however, they became convinced that the Bible teaches exactly that. I know this is a controversial issue among Christians, but that is exactly why it is a good example. The people I am talking about did not start out neutral on this question; they hated the idea of God's sovereign choice of those who will be saved. How did such a deep-seated preunderstanding ever change? Slowly. As they would encounter a passage that seemed to teach the doctrine of election, their initial response would be to interpret the passage another way. Their existing preunderstanding would prevail. Ultimately, however, the weight of the evidence would bring them to the point where they were reluctantly willing to reconsider their preunderstanding. Perhaps they were wrong to change their minds; I am not arguing that here. Whether right or wrong, however, their strong predisposition against the doctrine of election was ultimately no obstacle to their embracing that doctrine.

4. The search for consistency is more than a tool to check the accuracy of our interpretations. The goal of Bible study is to transform our understanding of life. What good is an incoherent and inconsistent worldview? The Bible does not give us a few isolated and unrelated rules for living; it gives us a window on the coherent purposes of God. When we "apply" what we learn in the Bible, we are seeking to rebuild our view of reality into one that is more accurate and consistent. Without the search for consistency, the Bible's message will be of little use to us. A later section of this book will have much to say about this important process.

CONCLUSION

UNDERSTANDING THE BIBLE requires integrity and skill. I know that some Christians resist the idea that skill is involved. It is not human skill but the Holy Spirit who imparts understanding, they would argue. Although they are right to emphasize the role of the Holy Spirit, they have misunderstood what that role is. The role of the Spirit is to bring about a moral revolution in the hearts of God's people. Because we have the Spirit of God, the integrity required for understanding—the willingness to know and follow the truth—is a growing reality in our lives. But the normal work of the Spirit is not to bypass the Bible and pour information directly into our heads. God has given us a book, and books must be read and interpreted. Being people of the Spirit does not change the fact that we must develop skill as good readers if we want to understand the Bible accurately.

The authors of this book hope to help you understand and develop the skills necessary for sound Bible study. We want to show you how to learn more about the Bible's language and culture, how to read carefully in context, how to consider alternative interpretations, and how to seek after a consistent and coherent view of the Bible and of life. We do not pretend that the process is quick and easy. These are skills to be developed over a lifetime, and not everyone will have these skills to the same degree. The quest for these skills, however, is a journey well worth making.

STUDY QUESTIONS

1. Consider the following verses from John 6:

> [Jesus said to His disciples,] "There are some of you who do not believe." For Jesus knew from the beginning who they were who did not believe, and who it was that would betray Him. And He was saying, "For this reason I have said to you, that no one can come to Me unless it has been granted him from the Father." (John 6:64-65)

Using your imagination, construct two explanations of the meaning of this passage: (1) from the preunderstanding of one who believes God chooses those who will be saved, and (2) from the preunderstanding of one who believes that salvation is a free human choice totally independent of God's choice.

2. Consider the following verses from Hebrews 6:

> In the case of those who have once been enlightened and have tasted of the heavenly gift and have been made partakers of the Holy Spirit, and have tasted the good word of God and the powers of the age to come, and then have fallen away, it is impossible to renew them again to repentance, since they again crucify to themselves the Son of God and put Him to open shame. (Hebrews 6:4-6)

Using your imagination, construct two explanations of the meaning of this passage: (1) from the preunderstanding

of one who thinks that genuine believers can lose their salvation, and (2) from the preunderstanding of one who
thinks that genuine believers cannot lose their salvation.

3. Review the five steps outlined in this chapter. In the light
of those five steps, suggest some specific strategies we might
use in pursuing the meaning of John 6:64-65. Do the same
for Hebrews 6:4-6. (After you have read the rest of the book,
you might want to try this question again.)

CHAPTER TWO

The Goal of Interpretation

"There's glory for you!"

"I don't know what you mean by 'glory,'" Alice said.

Humpty Dumpty smiled contemptuously. "Of course you don't—till I tell you. I meant 'there's a nice knock-down argument for you!'"

"But 'glory' doesn't mean 'a nice knock-down argument,'" Alice objected.

"When *I* use a word," Humpty Dumpty said in rather a scornful tone, "it means just what I choose it to mean—neither more nor less."

"The question is," said Alice, "whether you *can* make words mean so many different things."

"The question is," said Humpty Dumpty, "which is to be master—that's all."

WE HAVE ALL HAD the experience of hearing a particular passage of the Bible explained in one way by one respected, godly teacher and quite another way by another teacher who is just as godly and just as respected. Often the differences do not have any major theological or practical importance, but sometimes the differences are of monumental significance for the way we live our lives. This phenomenon demonstrates an important point: the Bible has to be interpreted.

Unfortunately, there is no God-inspired handbook that explains the principles for interpreting the Bible. Some argue that the Bible itself gives us clues as to how it ought to be interpreted. Jesus and the apostles often explained or revealed their understanding of Old Testament passages; surely, some argue, we can learn how the Bible ought to be interpreted from their example. While I would agree with this claim, we cannot simply expect the Bible to tell us how it speaks to us, because this expectation presupposes that we already know how the Bible speaks. This objection may seem silly, yet it is at the heart of many disputes about how we should interpret the Bible. One who claims that the Bible itself gives us clues to its interpretation assumes that we can, to a certain extent, understand the Bible implicitly, that we can understand the Bible as written words without further reflection on the set of rules needed to understand it. Is this assumption valid?

If the Bible is our guide to truth, then the question of how one makes sense of it is crucial: we must determine the principles by which God intends us to interpret it. Furthermore, in order to have confidence that our interpretations are valid, we must have good grounds for concluding that this particular interpretive approach is sound. This chapter will argue that such a set of principles exists and that we can have the utmost confidence that these are the principles God intended for us to use.

FORMS OF COMMUNICATION

COMMUNICATION IS SIMPLY a way of transmitting information from one person to another. Pictures are a form of communication. A circle with a slash through the middle, for example, has become a common symbol of negation on information signs. Body gestures are also a form of communication. Everyone knows what the nod of a head means. But the most prevalent forms of communication are based on human language. On the one hand, human language is a single phenomenon; on the other hand, there are many manifestations of it. First of all, there are many different languages used by human societies. They all share much in common, making translation possible, but each has its own lexical and syntactical rules. Then there are derivative forms, such as written language and Morse code. One could go on listing forms of communication, but my point is that every kind of communication has its own set of interpretive rules and its own distinctive "look and feel." We recognize the form by its look and feel and then interpret it according to the rules of that form. If we fail to recognize the form, we can only guess wildly at the proper interpretation.

If my wife says to me, "The kids are in the back yard," I do not ask myself what kind of communication she is using, nor do I puzzle over the rules of interpretation she expects me to employ. We have a substantial history of communicating with each other using language—in particular, English. When my wife speaks, she uses familiar words assembled into recognizable constructions. If, on rare occasions, I hear her use an unfamiliar word or an unrecognizable construction, I immediately assume that I either heard her incorrectly or she misspoke. When I interpret her sounds as spoken English, the resulting message nearly always fits well with the surrounding circumstances. Because spoken English is our normal means of communication, as long as my wife's utterance sounds like spoken English, makes sense as spoken English, and fits the circumstances, I have no reason to think that it is anything other than spoken English. I would not be able to prove beyond any theoretical doubt that she is communicating in spoken English, but for all practical purposes, I know it to be true.

Now let us look at a different example. A complete stranger wearing a beret and carrying a loaf of bread walks up to me and says with a heavy accent something that sounds approximately like "Come in the alley, you!" and walks on by. I expect this person to speak English, because virtually everyone I come in contact with speaks English. Two facts, however, make me wonder whether I should interpret this communication according to the rules I use to interpret my wife's messages. First, the way the stranger pronounces words differs from standard English pronunciation, and I cannot be certain that I heard the English words I thought I heard. Second, his actions and body language do not fit what I perceived to be the message. While it is still remotely possible that the stranger is communicating in English, these facts force me to question my assumption. My confidence is further shaken when I recall that the stranger's statement sounded a lot like a phrase I learned in first-year French class: "Comment allez-vous?" This phrase (which means "How are you?") better fits the circumstances and the pronunciation than my first guess. The preponderance of evidence, therefore, forces me to conclude that I should interpret the stranger's message according to the rules of spoken French rather than spoken English.

One final example will highlight the difficulty of understanding unfamiliar forms of communication. A dog walks up to George and says in an undoglike voice, "Drnk erom erango dzuz." This statement has no elements that George can identify according to the rules of English. Nor does it appear to be French. Because George has had little experience communicating with dogs, he does not know what to expect, and he cannot identify any recognizable elements according to any form of communication known to him. He is at a complete loss to interpret this message.

Now let us raise the stakes. George is told that the dog's message contains information that will save George's life. Understandably, George is desperate to extract meaning from the dog's utterance. After studying each word of the statement, he hypothesizes that it means "Drink more orange juice." So George drinks a gallon of orange juice and goes to bed in peace. Should George be so confident of his interpretation? One can see how, by supplying missing vowels, rearranging letters, and substituting similar sounds, the dog's statement could be transformed into the proposed meaning. But where did those rules come from? What justifies such manipulations?

This is George's wild attempt to make sense of the dog's proclamation; he has no reason to think that anyone has ever communicated using such a set of rules. We might accept such an interpretation out of despair and from lack of any better alternative, but we could easily be convinced of another interpretation. To end the suspense, I will tell you the conclusion of the story: George did not survive the night. The dog's message, in dog language, meant "Conduct a one-day fast." Not having heeded this warning, George died of orange-juice overdose, which, as you may well imagine, is not a fun way to go.

These whimsical illustrations make a serious and important point: we know how to interpret a communication by recognizing its form. Both the sender and the recipient expect messages in a certain form to be interpreted according to the rules of that form. If we recognize the form, then we know what rules to use in interpreting it. If we do not recognize the form, then we are at a complete loss. Therefore, if my wife appears to be speaking to me in English, I assume that this is so and interpret her utterance accordingly. This places certain constraints on the sender as well as the recipient. In order for com-munication to take place, the sender must carefully put the message into a form that the recipient can recognize following the rules of that form, and then the recipient, having recognized the form, must interpret it according to the rules of that form.

THE BIBLE AS ORDINARY LANGUAGE

THIS MATTER OF recognizing a form of communication has important implications for interpretation of the Bible. If we pick up a Bible and open it, we notice that it looks like a book. When we turn to Romans, for instance, it appears to be a letter: characters make recognizable words, which make coherent sentences. When we read it like ordinary language, it purports to be a letter written by Paul to a group of people in

Rome. In other words, it appears to be a piece of literature that we can understand by the same rules we use to interpret any other piece of literature. As we have already seen, if it has the look and feel of language and it makes good sense as language, we can assume it is ordinary language.

The fact that we are not looking at the Bible in its original language form does not threaten this assumption. Romans, for instance, was originally written in Greek: the Greek letters made recognizable Greek words, the Greek words made coherent Greek sentences. But although Romans was written in Greek and must be understood according to the rules of customary Greek usage, it is still a piece of literature written in ordinary language. People who know Greek are able to make sense of it as Greek literature, and they have translated it into English for us to read. The same is true for all the books of the Bible; they were all written in known languages and correspond well to other forms of literature from their time and culture. Therefore, although we cannot ignore the differences between literature of ancient times and that of our own time, the Bible appears to be in the form of ordinary literature written in ordinary language.

Three arguments support the conclusion that the Bible was written in ordinary language. First, we would expect God to communicate to man in a form that is universally accessible. Because God wants "all to come to repentance" (2 Peter 3:9), it would be appropriate for God to address mankind in a form that all can understand. Every human being uses language, and although there are many obstacles to overcome in order to make sense of writings composed in an ancient language from an ancient culture, the language of the Bible is, in principle, accessible to all.

Second, it is like God to condescend to our level of existence in order to express Himself in human terms. The most outstanding example of this is the Incarnation. God became a man in order to reveal His divine nature to the world. Jesus was fully man—He got dirty, hungry, and tired just like we all do—yet He was fully divine and sinless. It is appropriate, then, that God would incarnate His message to mankind in a human form such that the message was preserved perfect and uncontaminated while not being any less human.

Third, it would be uncharacteristically deceptive of God to present His message to mankind in a form that invites us to understand it as ordinary literature when it is really something utterly different. God has a track record of exhibiting behavior that is mysterious to our way of thinking, but He does not deceive. God would be cruel to offer us truth in a form so disguised that we could not recover it. We are justified, therefore, in concluding that the Bible was written in the form of ordinary literature.

BUT IS THE BIBLE *ONLY* ORDINARY LITERATURE?

FEW CHRISTIANS WOULD argue with the conclusion that the Bible is written in the form of ordinary literature. The vast majority of Christians regard the words and sentences of Scripture as words and sentences in ordinary language. Argument enters in when the assertion is made that the Bible communicates *only* as ordinary language. Some believe that the Bible can also communicate in other ways that yield more helpful and personal messages.

One prevalent variation of this position considers the Bible to be a catalyst for authoritative thoughts. You have probably all heard examples of this perspective: A couple deliberates about whether to move to a neighboring state or remain in their current place of residence. As part of their deliberations, they pray to God and search the Bible for guidance. As they leaf through their Bibles, they run across a verse that says, "Be content in whatever state you have been called" (1 Corinthians 7:20).[1] They take this to be God's advice for them and decide not to move to the neighboring state.

Now, it is important to notice that this couple did not treat this verse as ordinary language. They did not look at this verse with the intention of determining what it contributed to the argument of the passage. Had they done this, they would have realized that Paul was talking about states of being or, more specifically, positions of responsibility with respect to other people. That the English word *state* can refer to states of being and to political divisions within the United States of America is mere coincidence. Had the Greek word in the original manuscript been translated with the word *condition* instead of *state* (as, indeed, it is translated in the latest edition of the New American Standard Bible), or if we used the term *province* instead of *state,* the couple would not have found the same significance in this verse. The double meaning of the English word *state* allowed them to make an association that is otherwise foreign to the passage. This association did not come from a plain reading of the text.

Is there reason to believe that God uses the Bible to communicate with us in the way this couple believed the Bible communicated? We can all sympathize with the couple's dilemma. On the one hand, they want to do the will of God. Therefore, they want God to speak specifically to their situation. On the other hand, the Bible was written in another time and culture, and a plain reading of the text does not produce personal advice that answers their particular question. In an effort to coax specific guidance out of the Bible, they resorted to loose association. In this case their method produced a clear and direct answer to their question. But was this an answer from God?

God certainly is capable of communicating in such a way—that is not at issue. The issue is how *does* God communicate through the Bible, and how can we be certain we have heard the voice of God? Interpretation by this method of loose association is tenuous. If the couple had been reading

Genesis 12:1, where God said to Abram, "Go forth from your country, and from your relatives," what would they have decided to do? Which message would be authoritative—this one or the one from 1 Corinthians? How can this couple have any confidence they are listening to the Word of God instead of the vain whispers of coincidence? If you have ever used this method of interpreting the Bible, you have probably been plagued with second thoughts as you proceeded to act on what you believed to be God's advice. It is possible to assuage those doubts with a resolution to stop thinking about the decision any longer while proceeding to act on it. But avoidance and wishful thinking are not ultimately satisfying, and the doubts eventually return. As a result, this approach to the Bible has no way of giving us any kind of assurance that we have heard God speaking to us.

In our opinion, any attempt to understand the Bible as something other than ordinary language runs aground on the same shoals. Any meaning derived from the Bible apart from understanding it as ordinary language is guesswork. How can we know that we are hearing God? Could our hypotheses be nothing but the machinations of our own minds? With these kinds of doubts we cannot act boldly with the confidence that we are obeying the will of God.

We are left with the conclusion that the Bible was written in the form of ordinary literature and that it communicates to us solely as ordinary language. This may seem a rather trivial and unpromising conclusion, but it is actually very significant. The rest of this book builds on this conclusion. If the Bible is in the form of ordinary human language, then our task is clear. In order to learn to interpret the Bible, we must consider carefully the principles according to which ordinary human language operates. Having done this, we can then apply these same principles to the Bible. The next three chapters are our attempt to delineate these basic principles.

THE GOAL:
RECOVERY OF THE AUTHOR'S INTENT

BEFORE WE CAN set out the principles by which we ought to interpret human language, we must be clear about the fundamental goal of human language. It is to transmit information from one person to another. A speaker chooses words and grammatical constructions that he believes will best represent the idea he wants to convey to his listener, and the listener sorts through the linguistic and contextual clues to recover the idea the speaker set out to transmit. In most cases this happens so quickly that we do not even realize we are doing it. We seldom have difficulty when we are listening to someone speaking in our native language, but anyone who has spent time learning a foreign language knows how complicated this decoding process actually is. Despite the obstacles, the communication is successful if the message that the speaker wanted to transmit is conveyed to the listener.

An author's intended meaning is that idea or set of ideas that the author seeks to communicate to his audience by the words and syntactical structures he selects. It includes nothing more and it includes nothing less. The author may know much more about the subject than he indicates in his statement, but because he did not choose to put those thoughts into language, they are not part of his intended meaning. He may even know that what he is saying is not true, but if he wants to deceive the listener, he will choose language that conceals the deception.

For an extreme example in which a very short statement can be intended to communicate a great deal, imagine a one-year-old child standing in the kitchen and pointing to a glass of water on the counter as he says, "Unhh." This is not a skillful use of language. But if the child uses that utterance to get someone to hand him the glass of water to drink, then that "unhh" means "Would you please give me that glass of water to drink?" We can know the child's meaning by asking him or, in this case, by complying with the request. If this satisfies the child, then our interpretation was probably correct. Interpreting this child's utterance was possible only in the context of the situation in which it was spoken. The syllable "unhh" did not provide enough clues for anyone—except maybe the mother—to decode the statement. An adult speaker is better able to construct a statement that contains enough information for his target audience to correctly decode the message he intends.

We have all experienced situations in which a speaker makes a statement, a listener responds, and the speaker says, "Oh, that's not what I meant." In such instances the speaker's original statement was not successfully communicated to the listener. Communicating through language is a difficult process susceptible to distortion, but if both the speaker and the listener perform their tasks conscientiously, human language is an effective—albeit imperfect—form of communication. It does not matter whether the speaker is highly skilled or unskilled in the use of language. He may even misspeak entirely (my nephews used to say "smashed potatoes"). Regardless of such obstacles, if the listener derives any message from the statement other than the one that the speaker intended, then the statement has failed to achieve its goal of communication. Therefore, only one interpretation of a statement can be correct; all others are incorrect. The correct interpretation corresponds exactly to the message that the speaker or author intended to convey.

MEANING VERSUS SIGNIFICANCE

WHEN PEOPLE DISCUSS interpretations of texts, there is often confusion about two aspects of a reader's response to what he has read. On the one hand, there is the author's intended meaning. There can be only one definitive interpretation of the author's words: the meaning that the author intended to communicate. In this sense a statement can only "mean" one thing, no matter how many people read and interpret it. On the other hand, because every reader brings different experiences and knowledge to the text, the words of the author will have a slightly different impact on each reader. In this sense the meaning of the text will be different for every reader. I will refer to this subjective response of the reader as the *significance* of the text.

In order to clarify further the distinction between the *meaning* and the *significance* of a statement, we need to think a little more about the process of communication. Any idea can be expressed in a multitude of ways. This summer I had just finished putting up a fence when some branches fell from our cedar tree and crushed the fence. I could describe what happened in any of the following ways:

1. Some limbs fell from our cedar tree.
2. Some huge limbs fell from our cedar tree.
3. Some limbs fell on our fence and crushed it.
4. Some limbs fell on our new fence and crushed it.

Each of these sentences is true, but each will conjure up a slightly different picture in the mind of any reader.

The first two sentences are alike except for the addition of one word *(huge)* to the second. The first sentence gives no clues about the magnitude of this event. Without any further indications, the reader is unlikely to think of this event as a catastrophe. The addition of the word *huge* in the second sentence gives an explicit clue about the magnitude of the event. The reader does not know how big the limbs were, but he does know that the author considered the limbs to be unusually large. The second sentence, therefore, can be expected to communicate to the reader that this event was out of the ordinary.

The third and fourth sentences also differ by only one

word. The third sentence indicates a certain amount of destruction caused by the falling limbs, but the fourth sentence evokes feelings of pity from the reader (at least it should). The destruction of a generic fence is unfortunate; for all the reader knows, the fence was about to fall down anyway. The destruction of a brand-new fence is unquestionably tragic.

The author's selection of words and syntax is an important decision. A poor choice of words obscures the author's meaning; a good choice of words clarifies. A good author is a true craftsman. He is able to combine words in a way that engages and directs the thoughts of the reader. A skilled political speechwriter can make unpopular policies sound desirable to the vast majority of voters. A novelist can create images that seem to be alive in the mind of the reader. A good lawyer can make a criminal's actions seem innocent or justified. In order to create the desired effect, the author must have an excellent command of language skills and he must have a sound understanding of the target audience such that he can predict how they will respond to his words. Inept use of language or inadequate knowledge of the audience can render the statement incomprehensible.

There is a limit, however, to how well a speaker can know the mind of the listener. No speaker, therefore, can completely control the impact of a statement on the listener. A statement will invariably spark thoughts, emotions, and associations beyond what the speaker intended to evoke. This portion of the listener's response, which was not intentionally elicited by the speaker, is the *significance* of a statement.

The difference between the intended meaning of a statement and its significance to the listener can be a difficult line to draw in practice, but it is easily settled in theory. We need only ask the speaker, "What did you mean to communicate by this statement?" Assuming that he responds to this question precisely and carefully, his answer will settle the issue. If a speaker says, "The sun rose at 5:35 today," I may ask, "Did you mean that the sun rose at 5:35 *in the morning?*" He would answer, "Yes. I did not make it explicit, but that is what I meant." I may ask further, "Did you mean to say that the sun literally rose in the sky at 5:35, implying that the sun travels around the earth?" The speaker would probably reply, "No, I was merely using a figure of speech. I did not mean to say that the sun literally rose into the sky." However, the speaker could say, "I do believe that the sun revolves around the earth, but I was not making such an assertion in my statement. I was merely using a common expression to describe what happens at dawn." Therefore, the speaker is the one who can best tell us what he intended to say. In practice, though, we can often only surmise what the author of a written work intended to say. In such cases this kind of imaginary interview helps us conceptualize the difference between meaning and significance.

The significance of a statement can vary greatly depending on the interests and knowledge that the listener brings to its hearing. If Mrs. Bigsley announces to a group of friends and acquaintances that she has come down with a rare form of cancer, responses will vary. The friend who knows that cancer can be deadly will respond by becoming upset. The friend who knows that this particular form of cancer is easily cured will respond by being mildly disturbed. The sole heir to her multimillion-dollar estate will have a mixed reaction. The research scientist who has always wanted to study this particular kind of cancer will see an opportunity. The psychiatrist who knows that Mrs. Bigsley is a pathological liar will have a response of skepticism. Each of these listeners is interpreting the pronouncement accurately, but each brings a different set of interests to it. Consequently, even though there can be only one meaning of a statement, there can be many significances.

One nice feature of language communication is that we can generally assume that a speaker or author wants his words to be understood. When an author composes a statement, he tries to provide all of the clues that his intended audience will need to recover his meaning. When an author addresses an audience with whom he is very familiar, he can write tersely because there is already much shared knowledge. When an author addresses a less familiar audience, he must explain his thoughts in much greater detail. In both cases, however, the author attempts to provide enough clues for his intended audience to understand his meaning. Therefore, to the extent that we can reconstruct what knowledge and background the target audience shares with the author, we will be able to recover the meaning that the author intended to communicate.

OBJECTIONS TO THE GOAL OF FINDING THE AUTHOR'S INTENT

SOME HAVE DISPUTED the claim that interpretation of language seeks to recover the author's intended meaning. They claim that once an utterance is made it takes on a life of its own; it acquires meaning that the speaker did not have in mind at all. This position has three variations.

Literature as a Catalyst for Thought

The most radical variation points out that some literature—certain works of poetry—have been written without any intention on the part of the author to communicate specific content. Rather, the verse has been crafted to serve as a catalyst to help the listener's mind generate various thoughts. The words of the poem spark entirely different thoughts in the mind of each listener. This phenomenon is held up as an example of how language can work.

I do not deny that language can be used this way. Language is a wonderful tool for evoking images. I know little about poetry and even less about painting, but to me poetry seems akin to painting in that both are attempts to create an impression by evoking images. In a powerful way, poetry and painting can call to mind images and feelings related to our experience. But words can be combined in a way that does not relate clearly to our experience. Take, for example, this line from Bob Dylan's song "Visions of Johanna": "The ghost of electricity howls in the bones of her face." The response of the listener is much like that of one looking at a Picasso painting—the mind scurries around trying to make sense of it. If I, the listener, cannot put together a coherent mental image that could feasibly correspond to the one intended by the author, then communication has not taken place. I am not arguing that language is incapable of evoking an image in the mind of the listener different from that in the mind of the speaker, but when language is not being used to transmit the author's intended meaning, it is not being used for its primary purpose—to communicate.

Literature as a Learning Tool

Another variation of the view that a work has a life of its own goes like this: we do not really read books to find out what the author was trying to say; we just want to gain knowledge or understanding. When I read one of Plato's dialogues, for instance, my mind becomes actively involved in the logic of the disputants. As my mind is challenged and interacts with the statements of the speakers, it begins to explore territory that it has never traversed before. At the end of the dialogue my thinking has been greatly enriched by the experience. It is silly, this variation argues, to worry about whether all that I have learned by reading the dialogue was intended by Plato. I should simply rejoice in what I have learned.

There is some validity to this perspective. If I learn some things in the process of reading one of Plato's dialogues, it is unimportant to determine whether these things came from Plato or whether they were my own thoughts. This same claim can be made in much of our reading, because the authors have no authority over me. I am free to understand or misunderstand them according to my liking. But when something is authoritative, we must pay attention to the author's intent. Picture yourself reading a pamphlet describing tax regulations. Can you still be indifferent to the intent of the author and be satisfied with profound thoughts that occur to you as you read? Of course not. When we want to know what another person means, then his intent becomes important. When an author has authority over us, we want to know what the author means. This is why intent is particularly important in the interpretation of the Bible.

Literature for Enrichment
A final variation on the claim that a work has a life of its own is represented by those who assert that a good work of literature means more than the author said. In other words, a piece of literature will lay a fertile seedbed from which will sprout a rich variety of robust thoughts and images in the mind of the reader. Exactly what thoughts and images come up is beyond the writer's ability to predict. Therefore, each reader will have a unique response to a given work.

I do not dispute that this happens. A good work of literature is able to coax deep emotions and profound thoughts from the minds of a wide variety of readers. The result is a rich experience for the reader. But how much of it can be called communication? Only the core of information originated by the author can be communicated. The ideas and emotions evoked by this core of information originate in the mind of the reader; they were not communicated by the author. Any ideas the author's words cause that are beyond what the author intended to convey are outside the control of the author and are therefore not the product of communication. Once again we are bumping up against the distinction between the author's intended meaning and the reader's perceived significance of a statement. Only the intended meaning is under the control of the author and carries his stamp of approval. The significance of a statement to an individual listener is outside the author's ability to control, and it may or may not meet with the author's approval. Therefore, once again, we find the principle that language, when used to communicate, must be interpreted in such a way as to recover the author's intended meaning.

AUTHOR INTENT AND INERRANCY

THE OBSERVATIONS I have made about author intent are extremely important in light of recent discussions about biblical inerrancy. Some contend that the Bible is so riddled with errors of history and scientific fact that a position claiming the Bible is completely without error is embarrassingly untenable. Some of those alleged errors of history and science would evaporate if the interpreters, while seeking the author's intended meaning, would grant the biblical authors the same flexibility of language we all enjoy.

One alleged error is Jesus' statement that the mustard seed is "smaller than all other seeds" (Matthew 13:32; see also Mark 4:31). Empirical evidence shows that the seed referred to is not, in fact, the smallest seed; many seeds are smaller. Therefore, some argue, Jesus' statement is erroneous. But we need to ask ourselves whether Jesus meant that the mustard seed was the absolute smallest seed in the plant kingdom. It is naïve to contend that because Jesus said that the mustard seed is "smaller than all other seeds," He was asserting that there are none smaller. We often say things that do not mean what they initially appear to mean. I remember attending a high school basketball game in which, after the introduction of each of their players, the cheerleaders chanted the player's name and then the words "He's the best!" Imagine me rising from my seat and screaming at the top of my lungs, "Error! Five players cannot all be the best. 'Best' is a superlative indicating that no one is better!" Do you think the cheerleaders would have blushed in embarrassment at their blunder? Of course not. Everyone knows that when they said "best" they did not mean "better than absolutely everyone else"; they simply meant "very good." We must grant Matthew and Jesus this same flexibility in the use of language. I believe that Jesus merely meant that the mustard seed is small relative to other seeds, and His audience would have implicitly understood this meaning. In the terms of our imaginary interview technique, if we were to ask Jesus if He meant to assert that the mustard seed is absolutely, without exception, the smallest seed in existence, I am confident He would answer no.

Lest it appear that I dispose of all the apparent errors in Scripture with a facile "Aw, the author didn't mean that," let us use the interview technique on another passage. Genesis says that Seth lived 912 years. Let us imagine an interview with Moses, the author of Genesis:

> Me: "Does the exact age of Seth at his death have any significance for the theological truths we gain from Genesis?"
> Moses: "No."
> Me: "When you said that Seth lived for 912 years, were you asserting that he lived 912 years and not a year more nor a year less?"
> Moses: "I was asserting that, to the nearest year, Seth lived 912 years."
> Me: "Then if we could prove that Seth lived 914 years to the day, would it be fair to say that you made an error?"
> Moses: "Yes."

This example demonstrates that *what* the author asserts—not its importance—is at issue. We must determine, as best we can, exactly what the author claimed to be true. Whatever the author actually claimed to be true, no matter how trivial, should stand up to the facts. If it does not, then and only then can we say that the author made an error. In determining what the author claimed to be true, we must not interpret the language woodenly or mechanically. Language is like an artist's paintbrush—within certain constraints there is a great deal of freedom in how it is used. The interpreter must grant this license, which we will discuss in later chapters.

LEVELS OF MEANING

IT IS SOMETIMES argued that the Bible communicates several meanings on different levels simultaneously. This claim is ancient. Origen, a second-century theologian, insisted that the Bible has three discernible levels of meaning, corresponding to the body, soul, and spirit. Others have argued that the book of Esther, for example, should be interpreted on two different levels. On one level, the book describes the heroic deeds of Esther and her Uncle Mordecai; it relates a historic event but has little significance for our lives. Understood at another, more spiritual level, this same narrative is an allegory portraying the dynamics of the spiritual struggle that takes place within the hearts of believers. Interpreted this way, every statement within the book means two different things at the same time. God is certainly capable of doing such a thing, but did He?

The Russian author Fyodor Dostoyevsky wrote a novel that was interpreted by the critics as a malicious attack on a popular countryman. Dostoyevsky objected that the novel was not an allegory and he had intended no such attack. In *The Diary of a Writer* Dostoyevsky argued:

> Give me whatever you please . . . and I undertake to prove to you by the very first ten lines, designated by you, that therein is precisely an allegory on the Franco-Prussian War or a pasquinade on the actor Gorbunov—in a word, on anyone you please, on anyone you may insist upon.[2]

Dostoyevsky's point is well taken: any given work can be taken to be an allegory of virtually anything. In the absence of indications that the author intended a work to be read as an allegory and indications as to topic of the allegory, we do not have the author's permission to concoct allegories and attribute the resulting meaning to him.

Aesop's fables are allegories. These vignettes usually feature animals acting and talking like people. A fable describes the actions and statements of animals in situations with which people can easily identify and then concludes with a moral. One well-known fable tells of a fox that spied some delicious-looking grapes hanging from a vine overhead. They looked so good that he had to have some. He jumped to grab them in his mouth, but he could not quite reach them. He tried time after time after time but failed repeatedly. Finally, exhausted from the effort, he gave up and walked away. As he left he muttered to himself, "They were probably sour anyway." (This is the source for our expression "sour grapes.") One can easily see that this fable is not about foxes. It was designed to highlight one of the weird but commonplace features of human nature: when we fail to achieve something important, we tend to downplay the significance of such an achievement in order to save face. In case we missed the point, the fable concludes with a moral: "Any fool can despise what he cannot get."

There is a sense in which this fable works at two levels simultaneously. On the one hand, it describes the behavior of a fox attempting to get some grapes; on the other hand, it describes human nature in the face of failure. Is this, then, an example of two levels of meaning? I think not. What was the author trying to tell the reader? Was the author trying to tell us about foxes? If it could be undeniably proven that foxes never eat grapes, would this fact have disturbed the author? Of course not, because the author was not describing the behavior of foxes. If we insisted that human beings do not act like the fox, would the author have been disturbed? Yes, indeed, because this is the point of the fable. In other words, even a fable has only one level of meaning. The author used language to relate a fictitious story about an animal. But because the reader knows the story is a fable, he also knows that the author was really talking about human beings, not animals. So fables are not, in the final analysis, an example of multiple levels of meaning in language.

Possibly there could be special uses of language in which the speaker and the listener tacitly know that two meanings are intended. Puns are an example of language drawing upon two meanings at the same time. Many jokes derive their humor from double entendre. I remember from childhood a joke about a music conductor who accidentally stabbed and killed one of his musicians with his baton. The conductor was subsequently convicted of murder and sentenced to death by electrocution. Three times the electric chair failed to kill him, so according to a seldom-used law, they had to let him go free. As they were releasing him, the authorities asked why he was unaffected by the electric chair. He replied, "I guess I'm just a bad conductor." Whatever humor this joke has comes from the double meaning of the word *conductor*. Is the man claiming that electricity does not pass through his body, or is he claiming to direct an orchestra poorly? The way the joke is set up, both could be true. The listener is forced to do a double take as he weighs both possibilities—herein lies the humor.

But did the conductor intend to say both things with his single reply? Let us say you witnessed his release, heard his response, and were called to court to testify about what happened. On the stand, under oath, if you were asked whether the conductor attributed the electric chair's failure to the non-conductivity of his body, you would have to say yes. If you were asked the follow-up question as to whether he claimed to be a poor orchestra leader, would you not have to say no? The first meaning is a reasonable response to the question; the second is not. Puns, therefore, are not really an example of two meanings in one statement. They are funny because they are calculated to evoke a silly or unexpected association in addition to the intended meaning. This ambiguity is intended by the author of the pun. It sends his listener on a rabbit trail to explore silly, possible meanings, but it is not a part of the meaning the author intends. The listener keeps trying to make sense of the statement until he finds one that fits. At that point he stops looking.

Once again we return to our premise: the Bible is God's communication to man in the form of ordinary language. As speakers and listeners of ordinary language, we expect to find only one level of meaning, and we know the rules for recovering that one level of meaning. Even if we were told that there is another level of meaning, we would not know the rules for recovering that second level. In any statement, therefore, we ought to assume only one level of meaning— unless we are told by the author that there is another level and how to derive it.

THE INSPIRATION OF SCRIPTURE

TWO POINTS EMERGE from the above discussion about the nature of ordinary language: (1) the goal of the interpretation of ordinary language is recovery of the author's intended meaning; and (2) ordinary language acknowledges only one level of meaning. Earlier I argued that it is most reasonable to assume that the Bible was written in ordinary language. It follows that our observations about ordinary language will be true for the Bible as well. Therefore, the interpreter studying Galatians should try to determine what Paul, the author of that letter, intended to communicate (through his selection of words and grammatical constructions) to his target audience. This seems quite reasonable and straightforward until we recall that the Bible is a unique book—it is divinely inspired. Does not this unique situation raise the possibility that the Bible could have two levels of meaning, even though this is not a typical feature of normal human language?

It is not uncommon to hear teaching from the pulpit that assumes multiple levels of meaning. I suspect that many of these teachers have never formulated their justification for such a practice. But if they did, it would go something like this: "The Bible is a unique book. It was coauthored by God, so we can be sure that every passage is packed with theological significance. Because the plain reading of some passages—the meaning intended by the human author—does not yield profound truths, we must search out God's intended meaning, which is somehow hidden behind the human author's words." The expression often used to describe this phenomenon is "The biblical authors wrote better than they knew." In other words, God revealed messages to the authors of Scripture that they themselves did not fully understand but that they obediently recorded. The verses cited as evidence are 1 Peter 1:10-11: "As to this salvation, the prophets who prophesied of the grace that would come to you made careful searches and inquiries, seeking to know what person or time the Spirit of Christ within them was indicating as He predicted the sufferings of Christ and the glories to follow." Clearly, if the human authors of Scripture did not fully understand what they were writing or had a different intent altogether from what God intended to communicate, then we need to go beyond the human author's intent to gain the full benefit of the Bible.

Whether the fact of inspiration should change our method of interpretation depends on how we envision inspiration taking place. Frequently, when we think of inspiration, we conceive of something akin to the "dictation theory": God revealed His words to the biblical author, who wrote them down. In this theory's most extreme version, the human author recorded word for word what God dictated. This understanding of inspiration leaves the human author's mind, at most, partially engaged with the content of what he was writing. Paul could have been daydreaming about sunbathing on the Adriatic beaches when he penned the book of Romans. If this were a proper understanding of the process of inspiration, then the words on the page would not represent the human author's thoughts, and the interpreter would be wise not to seek the human author's intent.

But the dictation model does not account for what we find in Scripture. First of all, the books of the Bible appear to be the products of the human authors who composed them. Paul began and ended his epistles with personal greetings and comments. Even the body of the letter is laced with comments that appear to have been drawn from his personal knowledge of the people he was addressing. Second, the books of the Bible reflect the character and personal circumstances of their human authors. The Bible contains four narratives of Jesus' life. While it is probably true that the authors of these Gospels referred to each other's accounts in the process of composing their own, each Gospel is different, indicating the different personal circumstances and personalities of the authors. Third, and most significant, the books of the Bible claim to be the product of the human authors: Peter referred to Paul's letters; Jesus referred to the writings of Moses and Isaiah; Paul referred to the writings of the prophets. In every case the books of the Bible were considered the works of the human authors. In all these ways the Bible itself indicates that the human authors were the actual authors of their respective books. The dictation model cannot account for this fact.

A correct understanding of the process of inspiration must account for two claims that the Bible makes for itself: (1) the books of the Bible are the products of their human authors; and (2) the books of the Bible are the authoritative, totally inerrant word of God. These two claims are easily compatible if we recognize that God could have constructed the personality, personal experience, and circumstances of each biblical author in such a way that each author wrote exactly what God wanted him to write. In other words, God authored the lives of each of the biblical writers, who in turn authored books that were the direct result of the shape of their lives. In this way the individual books could reflect the personality of the human author while containing exactly what God wanted written down.

According to this understanding of inspiration, the intent of the human author exactly corresponds to God's intended meaning. To find the human author's meaning is to find God's meaning. There is dual authorship, in a sense, but the two authors have a single meaning. Thus dual authorship does not imply two levels of meaning.

REPORTED SPEECH

IN SPOKEN LANGUAGE we frequently relay messages of which we are not the authors. When this happens, the intent of the one speaking the words does, in a sense, become irrelevant to the process of interpretation. Let us say that a friend comes to me with the message "Your wife said, 'If you like it, buy it.'" For half of this sentence the intent of my friend is what I want to recover, but once I pass the word *said,* I know that the intent of my friend is no longer important; his intent was simply to relay the message accurately. It does not matter what my friend thinks "it" is. He may very well not know. I want to figure out what my wife, the original author of the statement, had in mind. So once again we find the rule that human language allows for only one intended meaning at a time. In the case of reported speech there are two authors communicating two intents, but within the language itself there are indicators to tell us whose intent we ought to try to recover.

This observation is helpful in responding to the claim that the prophets "wrote better than they knew." Where they were simply relaying dreams, visions, or divinely revealed pronouncements, the prophets may not have known the meaning of the things they wrote. In these instances we want to recover the intent of the real author of the dream, vision, or divine pronouncement, that is, God. But these instances will be clearly indicated by the language, typically with a phrase such as "The Lord spoke to me, saying, . . . " or "God showed me a vision . . . " Without such an indicator, the reader will naturally and properly assume that the one speaking the words was the original author of those words. So there can be two intents, in a sense, but only one at a time.

CAN THE AUTHOR'S INTENT REALLY BE RECOVERED?

ALL OF THE discussion about the centrality of the human author's intent becomes moot if it is beyond our ability to recover. Some, claiming that it is indeed futile, advance two arguments: First, they challenge whether the author's intended meaning can ever be fully extracted from his words. Second, they challenge whether we can even retrieve the words the author originally penned.

Ideas can be very complex and not easily reduced to words and sentences. Even the most skilled author sometimes struggles for words to express his ideas, forcing his reader to try to decipher the message. Some argue that this process, so fraught with difficulties, is rendered futile. While this argument perceptively points out the difficulties inherent in the use of language, it magnifies them way out of proportion.

Language is not a perfect form of communication. When we try to comfort a loved one or when an unfortunate misunderstanding takes place, we become acutely aware of language's inadequacies. Mental telepathy would be far superior, but I, at least, have not yet mastered that art. So we are stuck with language as a means of communication. In spite of its inadequacies, however, language is really quite serviceable. We put language to good use every day. I have written this whole chapter in words formed into sentences. You may not perfectly understand all that I have tried to communicate, but you probably have a fairly good notion of what I have been saying. As you read further into this book, you will understand even better. Critics claim that language is too crude a tool for communicating abstract ideas, and yet they communicate this argument using language. The claim that an author's intent cannot be extracted from language is a gross exaggeration of the deficiencies of language.

The futility of seeking the author's intended meaning in the study of the Bible is defended with a second argument peculiar to the circumstances surrounding the biblical text. Because we no longer have the original manuscripts but only copies of copies of copies in which many alterations were made in the process of production, the biblical texts that we have now are significantly different from the texts that left the hands of the original authors. Under these circumstances, some argue, how can we reconstruct the author's intended meaning?

Again this argument has an element of truth, but it loses all sense of proportion. We do not have in our possession the original manuscripts penned by the original authors. But we can be quite certain that what we do have is very, very close to the original wording. And most of the alterations make no significant difference in how one interprets the passages. Most of the disputed wording is on the order of the difference between *but* and *however*. If this is a major concern to you, I suggest you acquaint yourself with the issue by reading a book on the history and transmission of the biblical texts. All Christians ought to be aware of the problem, but I do not believe that it undermines the authority of the Bible.

The intended meaning of the biblical authors can be recovered. It takes work and careful interpretation to overcome the obstacles of time, culture, and language, but the obstacles are not insurmountable. In the following chapters we will spell out the principles of interpretation that we are convinced must be used to arrive at a sound understanding of God's Word.

STUDY QUESTIONS

1. Is the view presented here in harmony with "literal interpretation" of the Bible?

2. Historical narratives are particularly tricky when we talk about the distinction between meaning and significance. Read the story of the murder of Abel (Genesis 4:1-16). Describe the meaning of the text, and then describe the significance.

3. If a messenger brought me a message that was unclear, I would seek clarity by asking the author of the message, rather than the messenger, to explain. In what way is this analogous to the relationship between God and the human authors of Scripture? In what way is it not analogous?

CHAPTER THREE

Language
Conventions

"She's all right again now," said the Red Queen. "Do you know
Languages? What's the French for fiddle-de-dee?"
  "Fiddle-de-dee's not English," Alice replied gravely.
  "Who ever said it was?" said the Red Queen.
  Alice thought she saw a way out of the difficulty, this time.
"If you'll tell me what language 'fiddle-de-dee' is, I'll tell you
the French for it!" she exclaimed triumphantly.
  But the Red Queen drew herself up rather stiffly, and said,
"Queens never make bargains."

IT IS A SHAME that God did not see fit to write the Bible in
twenty-first-century English, the language I know best. If the
authors of the Bible had written in English, I would understand more easily what they were trying to communicate. If I
easily understood the language of the Bible, I could concentrate on understanding the ideas it presents. But God did not
write the Bible in English. The Bible is written in ancient languages that ceased to be used long ago: Hebrew, Aramaic,
and Koine Greek. Therefore, a great deal of work must go into
the study of these languages in order to understand the scrib-
bles on the page. Only then can we go on to figure out what
ideas the Bible presents and the relationships among those
ideas. The languages of the Bible, then, create a major obstacle we need to overcome.

Some would claim this obstacle has been overcome already.

Because many scholars have spent their lives studying the biblical languages and recording their findings, and because other scholars have studied these findings and have used this knowledge to translate the Bible into English, some say the work of translating the Bible is done. The Bible has been responsibly translated into English, and thanks to the efforts of others, we need no longer bother with the ancient languages.

Indeed, we ought to be thankful for those who have contributed to this effort. But no translation can be entirely adequate. You have probably heard the expression "It lost something in translation." The fact is, something is always lost in translation. When I first started studying foreign languages, I thought every language was basically like English; they simply used a different combination of sounds to correspond to each English word. I thought I could just learn a set of new words for each idea and I would be ready to jabber away with complete fluency in another language. (Oh, blissful ignorance!) Now, twenty-five years later, I am still trying to master my first foreign language. Much to my dismay, I discovered that every language packages ideas completely differently.

When I was in college, I spent some time in the Soviet Union studying Russian. Once while visiting Kiev, our group of American students was told that we were going to have a party with some of the local "youth." When I heard the word *youth*, I envisioned a group of college students. When we arrived, I was surprised to find a group of people, mostly men, in their late thirties and early forties. Now you need to understand that I am not one of the world's great partygoers—even my wife complains that I am hopelessly dull—but I have seen more life at an old folks' home than these "youth" were able to muster. The Russian word for "youth" is not the exact equivalent of the English word. Something was lost in translation.

Because there is no one-to-one correspondence of words and grammatical structures from one language to another, a translator is forced to take a more hazardous route. To translate from one language to another, the translator must determine what idea is being presented in the original language, and then he must express that same idea, as closely as possible, in the other language. But the translation will never be the exact equivalent of the original.

Furthermore, when the translator determines what idea is being presented in the original language, he is interpreting. If he misinterprets the statement in the original language, his translation will be even further off the mark. And if his translation is in error, you will not be able to discover the meaning of the original statement. Therefore, to depend on the work of the translator is to trust *his* interpretation.

I am not suggesting that the translators of the Bible are trying to mislead people. An enormous amount of work goes into translating the Bible. For most of the major English translations, much of this work consists of critiquing and revising tentative translations in an attempt to assure the highest possible level of accuracy. But the mere existence of differing translations of the same Greek and Hebrew manuscripts testifies to the difficulty of the undertaking.

The student who has learned the biblical languages can avoid the problem of distortion introduced by the translator. Ideally, every student of the Bible would learn the biblical languages. But let us put things in perspective: no one can personally collect, examine, and interpret every piece of evidence that could have a bearing on the study of Scripture; this is simply impossible. Everyone who does any research ends up using the scholarship of others and, consequently, trusting those scholars' work to some degree. The translator trusts the linguist; the linguist trusts the archaeologist; the archaeologist trusts the manufacturer of his instruments; and so forth. It is impossible, therefore, to study the Bible without relying on the work of others. Nevertheless, we need to be aware that many, many judgments are made by each person along the way, and some of them are hasty, misleading, or even downright wrong.

The fewer intermediaries we have between the raw data and ourselves, the less is the chance of distortion by others.

Ideally, each of us would examine all of the data individually. But that's impractical. Realistically, our responsibility is to minimize those intermediaries as much as time, aptitude, and other limitations will allow. For one person this will mean full-time study of Greek, Hebrew, Ugaritic, and who knows what all else. For another it will mean sporadic study of the Bible in translation. Neither is necessarily the better person; our value is established on another basis entirely. We just have different roles to play within the body of believers.

Whatever our particular roles, it is helpful for us to understand the limitations of translations. Just understanding the nature of language and the difficulties that the translators face means a little less dependence on the translator. And then we can take other steps to lessen our reliance on the translator still further. For example, even without knowing the original languages, the Bible student can undertake word studies, language studies, and genre studies.

In this chapter I am going to explain how language works and how we can determine the meanings of words and grammatical constructions. Earlier I expressed my regret that the Bible was not written in twenty-first-century English. That would have been nice, but it would not remove the need for word and grammar studies. In fact, such study is necessary in the close examination of a text no matter what the language. I recently became involved in a legal matter that hinged on the meaning of *own*. The question arose as to whether ownership requires clear title or whether possession alone is adequate. This can only be resolved by a word study in the relevant legal literature. The techniques I will describe are commonsensical and flow directly out of the nature of language, no matter what the language is. I am afraid that these studies will sound technical and tedious and will therefore be off-putting. They are not really so bad. In fact, some people find them enjoyable. But I will not try to persuade you of their pleasure value. Motivation is easily found in the significance they hold for understanding the biblical texts. I will demonstrate their significance by citing two examples.

Matthew 5:32 says, "Everyone who divorces his wife, except for the reason of unchastity, makes her commit adultery." Every English translation I have checked translates the Greek word *moicheuthēnai* as "commit adultery." The English word *adultery* implies complicity on the part of the woman. So the reader of this English rendition is forced to postulate that Jesus assumed that the divorce puts the woman in a position where she will be tempted to commit an adulterous act. A commonly noted implication of this rendering of the verse is that a divorced woman ought not remarry. But having done a word study on *moicheuthēnai*, I have concluded that the Greek word does not denote complicity on the part of the woman. This changes the whole complexion of the verse. On the basis of this information, I would paraphrase this verse this way: "Everyone who divorces his wife, except for the cause of unchastity, defiles her." Notice that the denunciation of remarriage has disappeared. So the word study makes a difference. Whether a person agrees with my understanding of the verse or not, it is an issue that hinges on a word study. Either I have done the word study well or I have not. My conclusions can be substantiated or refuted only by reviewing my word study.

Here is another example. In an article entitled "Does Male Dominance Tarnish Our Translations?" Berkeley and Alvera Mickelsen question the accuracy of the rendering of 1 Corinthians 11:3-12 in some translations. As part of their argument, they list the meanings of the word translated "head." They write, "A more common meaning was source, or origin, as we use it in the 'head of the Mississippi River.'"[1] Wayne Grudem responded to this claim with an article describing the results of an extensive word study on *kephale* ("head"). On the basis of his study, Grudem concluded, "Thus . . . we are left with no evidence to convince us that 'source' was a common or even a possible meaning for *kephale* in Greek literature."[2] The Mickelsens and Grudem cannot both be right. Thus the issue of male headship can be fully resolved only by a careful examination of the word-study evidence.

These studies are important. Interpretations and applications of biblical passages pivot on meanings of words and grammatical constructions. Lexicons and grammar books can help us in this regard, but ultimately our knowledge of words and grammar comes from a study of the language itself. An interpreter must know how this is done. Before I talk about this further, however, I need to lay some groundwork on the nature of language and how it works. The following discussion is a cursory survey, but I think it will be sufficient for our immediate purposes.

How Language Works

LANGUAGE IS THE means by which a speaker transmits an idea from his mind to the mind of another. The basic building blocks of language are words and grammar. Words are simply combinations of sounds that have ideas associated with them. If I say "caviar," you immediately envision a mass of salty, jellylike spheres. If I say "slug," you think of a slimy creature that you can find by tracking the silvery trail of goo it leaves behind. If I pronounce the word *purchase,* the exchange of money for goods comes to mind. Grammar takes us further. Grammar indicates the relationships among the ideas that the words represent. If I say the sentence "Wentals ladoned intap," you will not recognize any of the words (I hope), but there are some things that you can surmise. Whatever a wental is, you know that more than one of them did something. You also know what they did—they "ladoned." The ending (-ed) tells you that the action happened in the past. And finally, you can guess that the last word tells what was ladoned. But it could be that "intap" tells you *how* the wentals ladoned—quickly, slowly, daily, or whatever. Without knowing the ideas associated with the words, it is difficult to know exactly what the grammar indicates. Let us put the grammar together with words we know: "Slugs purchased caviar." Now it all makes sense. We can well imagine a group of slugs slithering into the local delicatessen, taking a few crisp bills out of their wallets, and buying a small jar of fish eggs. By the use of words and grammar, I have conveyed a thought (far-fetched though it may be) from my mind to yours.

When you stop and think about it, language has incredible potential. By using words and grammar, any thought that is in my head can be transferred into the head of another person. This is why language is called a form of communication. But language is an imperfect form of communication. The speaker takes his thought and puts it into a code consisting of words and grammar that approximates what he is trying to communicate. The listener deciphers the code and reconstructs, as best he can, the thought that the speaker had in mind. This requires work as well as cooperation between the two parties. The speaker must work hard at expressing his thoughts as clearly as possible. The listener must work hard at trying to understand those thoughts. And both must use the same code: they must assign the same meanings to words, and they must use the same rules of grammar. The greater the cooperation between the speaker and the listener, the greater the potential for true communication to take place.

The code of grammar and words that we use existed before we were born. We did not have any say in its formation. The code has all been decided by social convention. The set of language conventions I am using to write this chapter is twenty-first-century English. I know this language better than any other language, and I can understand most communications in this language with little difficulty. But for me to understand communications in another language requires a great deal of study. Every language divides the universe of all meanings differently and assigns different combinations of sounds to those meanings; every language has its own unique ways of relating those ideas. I have to learn the conventions of that language. Language conventions are what make language work. We will look at them more closely.

What Makes Language Work

GIVE ME ONE good reason why the combination of sounds spelled as *house* should mean "a building for human beings to live in." Why wouldn't another set of sounds be just as appropriate? Maybe *alabaster*. Or *plitzer*. Let us try a long word: *walomastulasinger*. Or if you prefer, a short word: *ti*. All of these sounds would work; take your pick. In fact, any combination of sounds would work. There is nothing inherent in the sounds that makes one combination of sounds more appropriate than another for this particular meaning. Any combination of sounds could mean anything.

A combination of sounds that can mean anything means nothing. A combination of sounds has meaning only in so far as a meaning has been assigned to it. The assignment of meaning to combinations of sounds is done by social convention. The same could be said for the assignment of significance to grammatical markers. If you're like most people, you were introduced to your set of language conventions by your mother. It did not happen formally. She just repeated each word in association with its meaning, time after time after time. She pointed to a bottle and said, "Bottle." And you pointed to the bottle and said, "Boddow." You began to understand that a particular set of sounds (or any reasonable facsimile thereof) signified a bottle. She pointed to herself and said, "Mama." And you pointed to yourself and said, "Mama." This response indicated that a few more lessons were necessary. But eventually you understood that she was called "Mama" and you began to use the word appropriately. The process continued until you were proficient in the English language. This is how you were initiated into the group of people that speaks English.

The formation of language conventions is a genuinely democratic process. As a speaker of English, you are a voting member in the process. Every time you use a word with a certain meaning, you are casting your vote in favor of that association. If enough people use the same word with the same meaning often enough, then the word *has* that meaning according to convention. If I hear the combination of sounds spelled as *dog* in reference to *Canis familiaris* often enough from enough people, I become convinced that this is the meaning associated with that combination of sounds. I can then use that combination of sounds with the confidence that others will know what meaning I intend to associate with it. The term "language convention" refers to this phenomenon. We assign meanings to all words, all grammatical features, and all genres in this way.

One must not conclude that language conventions, once established, are fixed for all time. Conventional features are added, subtracted, and changed constantly—all according to the same democratic process. For instance, we could create a new word right now. I have long felt that the English language is sorely in need of a word that means "to smother in mushrooms." Let us use the combination of sounds spelled as *smuroom*. If I say, "I want my hot dog smuroomed," I mean, "I want my hot dog smothered in mushrooms." Now, with a little help from all of us, we can make this word work. If enough of us will go out and use this word with this meaning, eventually so many people will know the word *smuroom* that we could begin to assume that when we use it, others will immediately understand what we mean. Words are added regularly to our vocabulary by this same process. In the last few decades many new words, such as *glitch, Xerox,* and *Ms.,* have worked their way into our vocabulary. We keep up with these changes in vocabulary by listening to others speak.

The meanings of words can change. The word *gay* is a good example. When I was young, the word *gay* described an emotional disposition. At that time, when I read the phrase "He was a gay young fellow," I knew the author meant the subject was a lively, happy young fellow. Since then, the word *gay* has acquired a different meaning: homosexual. Now if I encountered the phrase "He was a gay young fellow," I would suspect the author meant the subject was a young homosexual man. The meaning of the word has changed dramatically. It changed by the grassroots process described above.

Words can also fall out of use. People simply stop using certain words; therefore, the words are not passed on to the next generation. I remember hearing my father use the expression "full as a tick." A rather disgusting expression, I thought, imagining a blood-sucking insect buried headfirst in flesh, greedily kicking its feet to get closer to the source of blood. Later, I was pleasantly surprised to learn that people used to sleep on straw-filled mattresses called "ticks." Presumably the expression "full as a tick" draws on this meaning of the word. Why didn't I know this meaning of *tick?* We do not use ticks anymore; therefore, the word fell out of use. No longer a part of our active vocabulary, it will soon be erased from contemporary English. (I suppose now we will say, "Full as a futon.")

Thus far I have used the meanings of words as examples of changes that occur in language conventions. But changes occur in all language conventions, not just word meanings. For example, changes also occur in grammar. There used to be a tightly held distinction between adjectives and adverbs. For example, the word *quick* is an adjective. Therefore, we could say, "He has quick feet." The adverbial form is *quickly:* "He moved quickly to get out of the way." But recently, because of a growing tendency to use the adjectival form as an adverb, we hear, "He came here real quick." My fifth-grade

English teacher would have insisted on this construction: "He came here really quickly." In the past the forms *real* and *quick* were considered strictly adjectival, but the construction above required adverbial forms, thus the substitution of *really* and *quickly*. I read in the preface to a new edition of a dictionary that this shift is indeed common, and for some words, such as *fast,* this dual usage is now considered acceptable—a clear example of a change in grammar conventions. Obviously, then, language conventions change with time.

Language conventions also vary from subculture to sub-culture. It stands to reason. Because we learn language conventions by listening to others talk, the language conventions we learn are those embraced by our family, friends, fellow workers, and other persons with whom we associate. For example, in England the hood of a car is a "bonnet" (of all things). On the East Coast carbonated beverages are "soda," whereas we on the West Coast call them by their proper name, "pop." There are endless examples of differences in language conventions that, like "hood" and "bonnet," "soda" and "pop," relate to geography. Other factors also produce subcultures: religion, for example. It would not be out of place for some-one at a Bible study to say, "I enjoy the fellowship here." The speaker of this sentence would be referring to the camaraderie that he senses. Someone at a bar could sense a similar cama-raderie, but he would not use the word *fellowship,* for *fel-lowship* is not in the active vocabulary of the subculture of bar frequenters.

Language usage can even be idiosyncratic. People use lan-guage to express themselves, and because people are different, they use language differently. One day, at the conclusion of the first class in a quarter-long course I was teaching, a woman handed me a note containing a few questions and suggestions about the course, concluding with the sentence "I anticipate the class very much." Immediately, I was struck by the fact that I would never use *anticipate* in this way. I understood what she meant; I just do not use the word *anticipate* the same way. I use the word *anticipate* only to mean "expect." If I want to indicate eager expectation, I use the phrase "look forward to." I have another not-exactly-standard habit: I use the word *thoughtful* in two senses. Sometimes I use it to mean "considerate"; other times I mean "pensive" (a usage some people do not acknowledge). You can see that I have my own understanding of English language conventions as well as my own preferences. And you do, too. Our understandings and preferences differ slightly, but the language conventions we use coincide to an enormous degree with those used by all other speakers of English. This makes communication possible. If there were significant differences in the language conventions we consistently use, it could be legitimately said that we speak different languages.

But why do I have to be tied down to language conventions at all? Why couldn't I just strike out on my own? This is entirely possible. In fact, here goes: "Luxor ison allus sallwinden." It feels good to be unfettered by the constraints of social convention. But I have sacrificed something: communication. There is no way around it—to the extent that a speaker violates the rules of social convention, he risks not being understood. Unless the listener can use conventional clues to figure out what the speaker is saying, the speaker cannot be understood. For example, if I say, "According to the ghweter, which is held to my arm by a watchband, it is now 8:26," you can figure out what a ghweter is—but only because there are enough clues consistent with the rules of convention to determine what I meant. The word *ghweter* is no help; it communicates nothing.

We all sense that we have to use language according to convention in order to be understood. We can violate convention only in a context that is so clear that a listener can determine what we are saying in spite of the deviation. The purpose of language is communication. If we do not communicate when we speak, we are wasting our time and the time of others. Therefore, we speak in accordance with convention, and others do the same. When we interpret what others say, we naturally assume that what they say is formulated in accordance with language convention. As interpreters of the Bible, we must assume that a passage of Scripture was written in accordance with the language conventions of the time and place in which it was written, unless there is good indication that the speaker momentarily deviated from the conventions.

FIGURATIVE LANGUAGE

TO CONCLUDE THAT language conventions are well defined and restrictive would be a big mistake. We have seen how the speakers of any language are constantly nudging the boundaries of language conventions. But even staying well within the language conventions, a speaker has considerable latitude in the way he expresses himself. Language conventions are both imprecise and flexible; the two qualities go hand in hand. If each word could mean only one very specific thing, we would have to have an enormous vocabulary in order to talk to one another. Some words are more specific in reference than others, but every word is flexible. A number of words are so general in reference that they mean almost anything— words like *thing, interesting,* and *stuff.* But we need these words. I could not communicate all this interesting stuff without these things.

One natural manifestation of the flexibility of language is figurative language. Figurative language is not mysterious; it is simply a way of applying one or more characteristics of one thing to something else. If I wanted to say that my son is large and solid, I could say, "My son is a tank." No one would think I was claiming that my son is a heavily armored vehicle; they would know I was attributing some outstanding characteristic of tanks to my son. Given enough context, any listener should be able to know what characteristic I meant. If I were to say, "This course is a bear," the listener would know I was not claiming that the course and a bear are the same in all respects. The listener would know I meant that both the course and a bear have a characteristic in common: they are both difficult to cope with. Figurative language, then, juxtaposes two ideas in such a way that the characteristic they share is made obvious. That being the case, there is no trickery, no mystery. The meaning the author intended is plainly there, and any careful listener should be able to recover it. Figurative language is just one more weapon in the arsenal that the speaker uses to communicate more clearly. (Note the clever use of figurative weaponry language.)

Someone might ask, "But don't you believe we should interpret Scripture literally?" The word *literal* has two different meanings; my answer depends on which meaning the questioner intends. Literal can mean "nonfigurative" or it can mean "as the author intended." I do not believe we should interpret the Bible nonfiguratively. To believe this would be to envision Jesus as a wooden door, complete with doorknob, because He said, "I am the door" (John 10:7). I do believe, however, that we should interpret the Bible as the author intended. I am allowed to interpret words figuratively—but only when it is clear that the author intended them to be figurative. What is more, to fail to treat as figurative language what the author intended to be figurative is to misunderstand the communication.

Language, then, is based on social convention. We are all participants in a giant, silent conspiracy in which we all tacitly agree to use grammar and words in accordance with the way others use them. Therefore, we use language conventions when we speak, and we use them when we interpret. If either the speaker or the listener fails to use them, communication will break down. We need to keep in mind four facts about language conventions:

1. They evolve slowly over time.
2. They vary slightly from subculture to subculture and even from person to person.
3. The conventions of language have considerable flexibility.
4. Figurative language is a natural aspect of language, based on the association of ideas.

This concludes my brief explanation of the nature of language. The importance of this explanation may not be immediately obvious, but it is the foundation for what follows. A well-developed sense of what language is—and what it can and cannot do—will spare you a lot of interpretive blunders. If an interpretation of a passage is defended in a way that violates the nature of language, then it is wrong. Therefore, when we compare an interpretation of a text with words themselves, we must continually ask ourselves, "Can language do this?"

Before leaving this discussion, I will give one quick example of how the nature of language affects the interpretation of the Bible. According to one interpretive principle called "constant word usage," if a word has meaning X in one biblical passage, it will have that meaning in every passage where it occurs. Interpreters usually employ this constant-word-usage principle when interpreting symbolic language. Accordingly, because Jesus used the bird as a symbol of the Evil One in the parable of the soils (Matthew 13:3-9), the constant-word-usage principle tells us that a bird is always a symbol of evil. Therefore, when we look at the parable of the mustard seed (Matthew 13:31-32), we know that the birds that come and nest in the tree are representative of the Evil One. You can see the usefulness of such a principle, but is it consistent with the nature of language?

Consider the rain. It can be seen as something bad: it spoils picnics and softball games. Therefore, I could use rain to symbolize that which causes disappointment and sadness. But rain can also be seen as something good: victims of drought request rain in their prayers. Therefore, I could equally appropriately use rain to symbolize renewed hope. Furthermore, I could even use rain one time to symbolize disappointment and another time to symbolize renewed hope.

When we look at other passages of the Bible where the word *bird* is used symbolically, we see that it does not always symbolize the Evil One. In Hosea 7:12 the birds are symbolic of a helpless and naïve nation of Israel, whose desperate plans God is going to foil. In a passage that is very like the parable of the mustard seed (Ezekiel 17:22-24), the birds, if they are symbolic of anything, are symbolic of the lowly and powerless who are in need of protection. The principle of constant word usage does not hold up to examination of the texts, and it is not consistent with conventions of normal human language. Therefore, we must reject it as a valid interpretive principle.

Because normal human language is flexible, we must allow the biblical writers the same latitude we have. We cannot unilaterally impose restrictions on the biblical writers that are not inherent in the nature of language. Therefore, we are forced to determine the meaning of the symbol the old-fashioned way—from the context. But that is another chapter. Back to the task at hand.

USAGE AND MEANING

HOW DO WE determine what the language conventions are for a given culture at a given period of time? We observe the usage of language in that culture at that period of time. That is how you learned English as a child—you listened carefully to what others were saying and slowly learned the conventions. That is also how we have to reconstruct the conventions of dead languages.

Usage determines meaning. You can determine the conventional meanings of a word by examining the way it is used. If we understand this concept, we will be less likely to fall into a number of interpretive pitfalls.

Every Bible student can and should know how to investigate the language conventions of the biblical languages. Someone might ask, "Is it really necessary to research the language conventions of the biblical languages for oneself? Granted, a certain amount of independence from the translator is helpful, but there exist many large dictionaries and grammar books that record the results of many hours of linguistic research into the language conventions of the ancient Greeks and Hebrews. Surely these are better than anything an individual could do." As I have already indicated, there is an element of interpretation in all of this research; this is one problem. But there is a more significant problem: no dictionary or grammar book is complete. To describe the rules of grammar and list the meanings of words is extremely difficult. The most complete grammar book in the world can present only a rough approximation of the grammar conventions of a language. The biggest dictionary in the world cannot fully describe every word in a given language.

One might ask, "Even if a dictionary isn't complete, doesn't it do a very good job of describing the meanings of words?" A dictionary does a good job of clarifying what words mean for those who already know the language. But for those who do not know the language, it is woefully inadequate.

Try to explain the difference between the words *bottle* and *jar.* A jar is squat; a bottle is tall, with a narrower top. Thus, we say "mustard jar" but "ketchup bottle." I have a glass container on my desk. It looks a lot like a bottle—tall, with a long, narrow neck. Periodically, I empty all the change in my pocket into this container. I call the container my "money jar." I just cannot bring myself to call it my "money bottle." If a glass container is used to hold money, it is called a "money jar," regardless of its shape. What if I had a bottle-shaped glass container that held cookies? Would we call it a "cookie bottle"? Of course not. A glass or ceramic container used to hold cookies is a cookie jar, no matter what the shape. It would be difficult to find such information in a dictionary.

You cannot appreciate how inadequate dictionary definitions are until you have learned a foreign language. Native speakers of a language can refer to a dictionary for a brief description of a word's various definitions because they more or less know the word already. But the dictionary does not have a full explanation of the word's meaning. Dictionaries and grammar books are great road maps, but you do not know the territory until you have actually toured the terrain yourself.

The nature of all language conventions is that they are better observed than explained; they are best understood on the basis of personal experience. The rules of usage for any word are extremely complex. Even when the rules are laid out, they are incomplete. And when they are described as fully as possible, they are often incomprehensible. Because of this complexity, word studies, grammar studies, and genre studies are advisable. But even if you never do one of these studies yourself, you still need to understand the limitations and difficulties encountered by scholars who do undertake them and on whose scholarship you rely.

WORD STUDY: JAMES 5:13-20

LET US PUT some of this theory into practice. Because we are looking at James 5:13-20 throughout this book, we might as well select a word or two from that passage to investigate. But which words? The first step in any word study is choosing a particular word or words to look into. Any word is worthy of investigating further. If we had unlimited time, doing word studies would be one way to fill it. But some of us do not have unlimited time; therefore, we have to be selective.

Some words are more crucial to the interpretation of a passage than others. How do I know which ones are critical? I ask myself two questions. First, *Do any of the words seem out of place in this context?* If they do, I may not understand the full meaning of the word. For the second question, I need a little imagination: *If I shifted the meaning of any given word, would the meaning of the passage change?* You might think that if you changed the meaning of any word, the meaning of the passage would change. Not so.

What if the word translated "rain" in James 5:17-18 really meant "pollinating bees"? Then these verses would read:

> Elijah was a man with a nature like ours, and he
> prayed earnestly that there might not be pollinating
> bees, and there were not pollinating bees on the
> earth for three years and six months. Then he
> prayed again, and the sky poured pollinating bees,
> and the earth produced its fruit.

The argument of the passage would not change. We need to know only that the word refers to a natural event. Clearly, James was saying that Elijah influenced the natural forces through prayer. For this passage, a fuller understanding of the word for "rain" would not be helpful.

On the other hand, the word translated "sick" in verse 14 is at the heart of the argument. James was commanding the one who was "sick" to call on the elders. How do we know to whom he was speaking? Our understanding depends on the meaning of the Greek word translated "sick."

Astheneō: "Sick" or "Weak"?

To do a thorough word study starting from scratch is difficult. Investigating a word is much easier when we have one particular question about the word in mind. We know that sickness is the precondition for someone calling the elders. Therefore, we will focus our attention on this one question: *To what extent, if any, does the field of meaning of the Greek word vary from that of the English word* sick?

First, we must chart out the field of meaning of the English word. A word's field of meaning is the set of all possible meanings according to the conventions of the language. Webster's Dictionary lists the following meanings for the English word *sick,* moving from most common to least common: (1) afflicted with ill health; (2) affected with nausea; (3) deeply affected with some distressing feeling; (4) mentally, morally, or emotionally deranged; (5) characteristic of a sick mind; (6) gruesome, sadistic; (7) of, pertaining to, or for use during sickness: sick benefits; (8) suggestive of sickness, sickly; (9) disgusted; (10) not in proper condition, impaired; (11) failing to sustain adequate harvests of some crop: wheat-sick soil; (12) idiomatic use—exasperated and weary. These, then, are the approximate boundaries of the field of meaning of *sick.*

Second, we must find out what the Greek word translated "sick" means. We are interested in the Greek word because it is the word the author used. In interpretation we want to recover the *author's* intent; therefore, we need to know the meanings of the words he picked, not the meanings of the words the translator picked. If you know Greek, you should have no trouble finding the Greek word in a Greek New Testament. If you do not know Greek but you do know the Greek alphabet, you can find the word in an interlinear New Testament. (An interlinear New Testament is the Greek text with a wooden English translation under each line.) "But I don't know *anything* Greek!" you exclaim. Never fear. Using an exhaustive concordance to the Bible, you can find the correct Greek word without knowing any Greek whatsoever.[3]

Astheneō is the Greek word translated "sick." How do we find out what this word means? We could break the word down into meaningful morphemes. A morpheme is the smallest unit of meaning in language. For example, the English word *dependable* has three morphemes: *de-*, meaning "down or from"; *pend-*, meaning "hang"; and *-able*, meaning "capable of being." If we put these morphemes together, *dependable* means "capable of being hung from"; in other words, "trustworthy." Similarly, we can break down *astheneō*. The root word is from *sthenos*, which means "strength." The prefix, *a-*, is a negating particle. Putting these parts together, the word should mean "not strong." This is all very nice but not really very helpful. *The etymology, or ancestry, of a word is not a reliable guide to its meaning.*

As a speaker of English, how much do you concern yourself with the etymology of a word? Probably not at all. The expression *goodbye* comes from "God be with ye (you)." But *goodbye* does not mean "God be with ye." It means "This meeting has come to an end and we are parting." Etymologies are interesting and fun, but they have a fatal limitation for our purposes—they can help *explain* the meaning a word has, but they cannot *predict* the meaning. Let us try another example. The nouns *wonder* and *awe* are nearly synonymous. Notice what happens when we add the suffix *-ful* to each word. The resulting words, *wonderful* and *awful,* are nearly antonyms. Etymologies are really only helpful once we know what the word means. Having said this, I must admit that if we have no other evidence as to the meaning of a given word except etymology, determining the meaning on the basis of etymology is better than blind guessing.

Etymology does not determine meaning; usage determines meaning. Let us look at the way *astheneō* is used in the New Testament. With your concordance, you can find all the places in the New Testament where this word occurs, a total of thirty-seven:

Matthew 10:8	John 11:2	2 Corinthians 11:21
Matthew 25:36	John 11:3	2 Corinthians 11:29
Matthew 25:39	John 11:6	2 Corinthians 12:10
Mark 6:56	Acts 9:37	2 Corinthians 13:3
Luke 4:40	Acts 19:12	2 Corinthians 13:4
Luke 7:10*	Acts 20:35	2 Corinthians 13:9
Luke 9:2*	Romans 4:19	Philippians 2:26
John 4:46	Romans 8:3	Philippians 2:27
John 5:3	Romans 14:1	2 Timothy 4:20
John 5:7	Romans 14:2	James 5:14
John 5:13*	Romans 14:21*	
John 6:2	1 Corinthians 8:11	
John 11:1	1 Corinthians 8:12	*in some manuscripts

We should examine every one of these passages, but for the sake of expediency, I will comment on just a few of them. Please look up each of the verses that I talk about. Then make your observations before reading what I have to say.

> While the sun was setting, all those who had any who were *sick* with various diseases brought them to [Jesus]; and laying His hands on each one of them, He was healing them. (Luke 4:40, emphasis added)

This verse talks about people who were "sick with various diseases." The added phrase, "with various diseases," clarifies the cause of the "sickness." The phrase does not tell us which diseases cause sickness, but it does link the ideas of sickness with "disease." The word *astheneō* seems to be used this way throughout the Gospels. This corresponds well with the first definition of the English word *sick*.

> In these [porticoes] lay a multitude of those who were *sick*, blind, lame, and withered. (John 5:3, emphasis added)

There are lots of ways to describe an array. One way is to list a number of different things in the array. The members of the list can be completely distinct from each other or they can overlap. I could say, "Into the room walked senators, lobbyists, and businessmen." In this sentence there are three distinct classifications of people: senators, lobbyists, and businessmen. Another way to describe an array is to characterize the array in general and then clarify it with examples: "Into the room walked men of distinction: senators, lobbyists, and businessmen." To decide which kind of list one is looking at is often tricky. It would appear that the list in this verse is composed of members that do not overlap. If so, then *astheneō* would not include blindness, lameness, nor witheredness and would resemble the English word *sick* in this respect. But this conclusion is not definite.

> The sisters sent word to Him, saying, "Lord, behold, he whom You love is *sick.*" (John 11:3, emphasis added)

This verse is in the account of the raising of Lazarus. The sisters reported to Jesus that their brother was sick. Clearly, they believed their brother's illness was serious and quite possibly was going to be fatal. Therefore, the word *astheneō* does include serious illnesses. This usage is well substantiated (see also John 4:46; Philippians 2:26-27).

> Handkerchiefs or aprons were even carried from [Paul's] body to the *sick,* and the diseases left them and the evil spirits went out. (Acts 19:12, emphasis added)

This is tricky. Was Luke describing the same event in two different ways? That is, did those who were sick experience the departure of the disease, which is the same as the departure of the evil spirits? If so, then disease was accompanied by demon possession. Or was Luke saying that there were those who were "sick" from diseases and there were others who were "sick" from evil spirits? In either case it is possible that the condition caused by demon possession was called "sickness." Because our culture does not generally recognize demon possession as a genuine phenomenon, it is difficult to say whether or not this use of *astheneō* would be in accordance with our use of the word *sick*.

Twice now I have reached conclusions that are tenuous. This is unavoidable when doing word studies.

> Without becoming *weak* in faith [Abram] contemplated his own body, now as good as dead since he was about a hundred years old, and the deadness of Sarah's womb ... (Romans 4:19, emphasis added)

This is interesting. The verse says Abram did not become "sick" in faith. Again, we have a phrase that specifies the kind of sickness being talked about. My translation even chooses another word to translate *astheneō: weak*. And rightly so. We do not use the word *sick* to refer to a failing or a lack of faith. We use the word *weak*. This meaning is a definite departure from the field of meaning of the English word *sick*. There are other places in the New Testament where *astheneō* is used in the same sense: Romans 14:1 and 1 Corinthians 8:7,9,12.

> You are seeking for proof of the Christ who speaks in me, and who is not *weak* toward you, but mighty in you. (2 Corinthians 13:3, emphasis added)

Another problem one faces when doing word studies is the considerable amount of work often necessary to interpret the entire passage where the word appears. This makes some word studies very time-consuming. This passage is one that is not immediately clear. I only want to point out that this verse contrasts "weak" *(astheneō)* with "mighty."

There we have a whirlwind tour of the word *astheneō*. The word is not the exact equivalent of our word *sick*. Basically, it seems to mean "weakness." Then, by extension, its field of meaning includes one of the most common manifestations of weakness, namely, sickness from disease. The meaning of the word may not include various infirmities, such as blindness, lameness, and withering. It may include the condition that accompanies demon possession. Nevertheless, the word's meaning is not confined to physical weakness; it can also refer to spiritual weakness, that is, weakness with respect to faith. We must keep this field of meaning for *astheneō* in mind when we look at the passage in James.

If we want to look at more evidence for the meaning of *astheneō*, there are a few things we can do. First, we can look at the Septuagint. A few centuries before the New Testament was written, the Old Testament was translated from Hebrew into Greek; this translation is called the Septuagint. A lot can change in a language over a few centuries, but more stays approximately the same. Therefore, with the help of concordances, we can include passages from the Septuagint in our investigation.

Second, we can check classical Greek sources. Although most classical Greek sources are removed further in both time and culture from the New Testament than the Greek of the Septuagint, they can nevertheless be helpful. Checking classical Greek sources would make our word study more complete and more reliable.

Third, we can look at words related to *astheneō*. Often closely related words have similar meanings. In our case we could check all of the occurrences of the noun form *astheneia* or the adjective *asthenēs*. This, too, will increase our evidence, but we pay for our increased data with increased complexity. When a prefix or a suffix is added to a word, a new word is formed. This may sound trivial, but it is not. Every word has its own network of ideas. When a syllable is affixed to the word, the resulting network of ideas is not simply the sum of the two parts. The word *suggest* means "mention something to consider." The word *suggestive* is just the adjectival form of the same word. But "to suggest something" and "to say something suggestive" are phrases with very different connotations. The same thing could be said for *awful* and *awfully*. If we include related words in our word study, we must be on the lookout for this kind of shift in meaning as prefixes and suffixes are added or taken away.

Our initial assignment was to try to stake out the field of meaning of the word *astheneō*. We have done that. We discovered that its field of meaning is similar to that of the English word *sick* in some respects but different in others. In particular, the Greek word is broader and centers upon the concept of weakness. It is especially interesting to note that *astheneō* can be used when talking about weakness with respect to faith.

This presents us with an interesting situation. In verse 14 of chapter 5, James told one who was *astheneō* to call for the elders. Then James referred to this same person as "the one who is sick" in verse 15. But in verse 15 James must have used a different word, because the verse was not listed with all the occurrences of *astheneō*. Therefore, even though *astheneō* can mean spiritual weakness, if James went on to specify that the problem at hand was physical weakness, then sickness was indeed the issue. On the other hand, if the word he used in verse 15 will grant the same latitude as *astheneō,* then James could still have been talking about spiritual weakness. Therefore, we need to take a look at the word James used in verse 15.

Kamnō: "Sick" or "Weary"?

Using the same procedure we used with "sick" in verse 14, we determine that the Greek word James used in verse 15 is *kamnō*. Continuing to use the concordance, we find that this word occurs only three times in the New Testament: Hebrews 12:3, James 5:15, and Revelation 2:3 (in some manuscripts).

Let us look at the usage of the word *kamnō* to see if its meaning has the same latitude as that of *astheneō*.

> Consider Him who has endured such hostility by sinners against Himself, so that you will not grow *weary* and lose heart. (Hebrews 12:3, emphasis added)

Clearly, the author of Hebrews was not talking about physical weakness in this verse. In fact, the subject is weariness that leads to losing heart—spiritual weariness, a wavering in faith. Notice also that the verse encourages the listeners to "consider Him who has endured . . . , so that you will not grow weary." This implies that *kamnō* is a failure to endure. For this reason it has been translated "grow weary."

If we exclude James 5:15 for the moment, there are no passages where *kamnō* means "to be sick." This does not prove that the word does not include that meaning. We only looked at one verse, and one verse a conclusive word study does not make. In fact, if you look at a lexicon, you will see that there are extrabiblical sources that use *kamnō* in the sense of "sick."

The Word Study Concluded

Our study shows that both words share the meaning "to be sick," but they appear to get there by different routes. *Astheneō* means "to be weak," and one form of weakness is sickness. *Kamnō* means "to grow weary," and one form of weariness is sickness.

This concludes our quick look at two of the keywords in our passage. What have we learned? Both words are translated by the English word *sick*. But now that we have looked at the usage of the Greek words, we know that the field of meaning for *sick* does not exactly match the field of meaning for *astheneō* or *kamnō;* both of the Greek words have meanings that extend into areas that are not included in the meaning

of the English word *sick*. The Greek words have the central idea
of "weakness" or "weariness," with "sickness" being one specific form of weakness. Now we must go back and look at our
passage and wrench our thoughts away from the images produced by the word *sick*. We need to look at the passage through
the eyes of the Greek readers. When we ask ourselves what
condition James was referring to, we must keep in mind the full
range of possibilities embodied in the Greek words. Only a
closer inspection of the context can pinpoint the exact meaning
the author intended. This is the topic of the next chapter.

SOME COMMENTS ON WORD STUDIES

ON THE BASIS of the preceding word study, we need to keep
in mind a few maxims when doing future word studies. The
list that follows is by no means comprehensive, but it hits the
high spots.

1. Usage determines meaning. How a word was used at the
time an author wrote is the only reliable kind of data we can
use to discover what a word means. Although we can consider other kinds of evidence to determine the meaning of a
word, word usage is by far the weightiest. Other kinds of data
mentioned frequently are etymologies and cognates (related
words in closely related languages). Both etymologies and cognates are of limited value and need to be used with caution.

2. The more data, the more reliable the conclusion. One of
the worst mistakes we can make is to jump to a conclusion for
which there is little support. Look at Genesis 3:16, noting especially the word *desire (teshuqah)*. Is this "desire" a healthy, natural desire, or is it a part of the curse—a perversion of the
way things should be? This word occurs only three times in the
Old Testament. In Genesis 3:16 the word is used with the
preposition *'el*. "Desire" is used the second time, again with
the preposition *'el*, in Genesis 4:7, where the one with the
desire is a personification (animation?) of sin. We naturally see

this desire as evil, a desire to consume. "Desire" is used the third and last time in Song of Solomon 7:10: "I am my beloved's / And his *desire* is for *['al]* me" (emphasis added). Here, "desire" is clearly a loving desire.

We can explain what we see in two ways. "Desire" could have either a negative or a positive connotation in biblical Hebrew, depending on the preposition. If the preposition is *'el*, the connotation is bad; if the preposition is *'al*, the connotation is good. Just as possible, however, the word could be neutral in connotation, and the choice of preposition does not alter that fact. (Note that with some words *'el* and *'al* can be used interchangeably, without any apparent change in meaning; for example, with *naphal*.) Which explanation is more likely the correct one? I do not know; there is not enough data. The word study will not be able to dictate how we interpret Genesis 3:16. The prudent thing to do is to treat the word *desire* as a neutral term and look for other clues in the passage to tell us whether this desire is good or bad.

3. The further afield we search for data, the less valuable that data is. Because we know that we need as much data as possible, we go reaching for data anywhere we can. But with each desperate grasp, we get further and further from the language convention of the author. Remember, as we move away from the time and culture of the author, the social conventions change more and more. For this reason, word studies done to interpret a passage in the New Testament are initially confined to the data from the New Testament (and sometimes more narrowly to the data from that particular author).

Studying related words runs the same risk of departing from the language convention of the author. All words carry their own baggage, and even related words can develop very different nuances. This does not always happen, but the fact that it happens at all means that we must beware.

4. It is a mistake to confuse what the word contributes to the context with what the context imposes on the word. One of the most difficult aspects of word studies is distinguishing how the word helps us understand the context from the impact the context has on the word. Example: I am researching the word *bliband* and I encounter the sentence "Harry's chauffeur drove me to his bliband." From the rest of the context I know that Harry lives in a bliband. I can surmise that Harry is wealthy from the fact that he has a chauffeur. But is *bliband* like the word *mansion,* reinforcing the idea of wealth, or is it a more general word like *house,* which does not have the connotation of wealth? To tell whether or not the word *bliband* connotes luxury is difficult. We would need to see other occurrences of the word to know for sure. When we do word studies on uncommon words, we are tempted to stretch the conclusions of the word study beyond what is reasonable.

5. Word studies are helpful but seldom decisive in resolving interpretive issues. Word studies are not a magic cure-all. But they do help us in two significant ways. First of all, they eliminate those interpretations that are generated by the English translation but that are not compatible with the Greek meanings. Second, they help us see interpretive options that were invisible to our English-oriented word associations. Some word studies provide dramatic eye-opening insights; others fail to turn up any particularly enlightening information. You never know how helpful a word study will be until you have done it.

OTHER LANGUAGE CONVENTIONS

IN PRINCIPLE WE can investigate any language convention in the same manner that we study word meanings. In practice this is more difficult. It is more difficult to locate occurrences of a given grammatical feature than occurrences of a given word. However, computers are changing this. In the future, grammar studies will be as feasible as word studies.

Another language convention even harder to investigate is literary genre. *Genre* indicates the kind of literature—novel, poetry, historical narrative, limerick, or whatever. Genre is important because each genre creates it own unique set of expectations. If I begin a story with "Once upon a time . . . ," you already know several things about what I am going to say, including the ending: "And they lived happily ever after." On the other hand, if a text begins by saying, "I, Joe Jones, do hereby . . . ," you immediately recognize a legal document and bring a completely different set of expectations to what follows. Therefore, identifying the genre is critical to the interpretive process. Unfortunately, we do not have an abundance of literature dating to the time and culture of the biblical texts that would allow us to analyze the different genres then in use. Nevertheless, an interpreter must be cognizant of the significance of genre and take it into account.

CONCLUSION

WHAT I HAVE presented in this chapter makes Bible study look like a lot of work. It is. Much of the work is tedious and time-consuming. But for good Bible study to take place, it has to be done. No one can do all the work that needs to be done, but everyone must do what he can. We need to be as biblically literate as our time, abilities, and interest will allow. And part of being biblically literate is knowing what kind of research goes into good Bible study; only then can we have any chance of assessing the results of such research critically. Even if you never do your own word study, you might use a lexicon or a grammar book. And even if you never use a lexicon or grammar book, you will use a translation. We must be aware of the kinds of difficulties that scholars face when they do their work; otherwise, we cannot use their books critically.

STUDY QUESTIONS

1. In order to answer this question, you will need to find information about the meaning of a Greek word. There are

many tools you can use to do this. Before asking the question, I will illustrate one way by looking up in *The New American Standard Exhaustive Concordance* the word *sick* used in James 5:15.

   a. Step 1: determine the word used in the original language.

      Looking up the word *sick* in the concordance, we find that the citation for James 5:15 has the number 2577 next to it. This is called the Strong's number. A man named Strong assigned a number to every Greek word used in the New Testament. This is handy for those who cannot read Greek. (The Strong's number can be found in concordances, in special "word study" Bibles, in Bible software, and probably other places as well.) Looking up number 2577 in the back of the concordance shows us that James used the word *kamnō*.

   b. Step 2: find the other places in the Bible where the word is used.

      If we were using Bible study software, we could just punch a button and have the computer generate a list of all the verses using the word *kamnō*. Using the *New American Standard Exhaustive Concordance* is a little more complicated. The Greek dictionary in the back tells us that the word is *kamnō,* but how do we find all the places where *kamnō* is used? We do that by following some clues in the dictionary itself. The citation for *kamnō* includes this cryptic comment: "grow weary (1), sick (1)." This tells us that NASB translated *kamnō* once as "grow weary" and once as "sick." We know that James 5:15 is the one place it is translated as "sick"; where does NASB translate *kamnō* as "grow weary"? Well, let us go back to the concordance and look up the word *weary*. We find many verses that use the English word *weary*, most of which are in the Old Testament. The long list does not faze us, however, because each citation is marked with the Strong's number of the original word. All we have to do is scan down the list and find number 2577, which happens to be in Hebrews 12:3. The tediousness of this process may inspire you to invest in some Bible study software or, even better, to learn Greek.

James 1:13 says, "Let no one say when he is tempted, 'I am being tempted by God.'" What is the Greek word translated as "tempted"? Where else is it used by James? What is the range of meanings it might have? What does James mean by it in chapter 1? Use what you have learned about this word in James to critique the Revised Standard Version translation of this word as "tempt" in Matthew 4:7.

2. Is Genesis 1–12 all the same genre? How do you know?

3. In order to interpret, you must do word studies. In order to do word studies, you must interpret. Is this a hopelessly vicious cycle?

CHAPTER FOUR

Context and Coherence

"I beg your pardon?" said the Mouse, frowning, but very politely: "Did you speak?"

"Not I!" said the Lory hastily.

"I thought you did," said the Mouse. "—I proceed. 'Edwin and Morcar, the earls of Mercia and Northumbria, declared for him; and even Stigand, the patriotic archbishop of Canterbury, found it advisable—'"

"Found *what?*" said the Duck.

"Found *it,*" the Mouse replied rather crossly: "Of course you know what 'it' means."

"I know what 'it' means well enough when *I* find a thing," said the Duck: "it's generally a frog or a worm. The question is, what did the archbishop find?"

THE EMBATTLED READER OF this book may be wondering if understanding the Bible is possible at all. You have been told that our preunderstanding can drastically affect what we see in a text. You have discovered that words are pliable things that can have many different meanings. Furthermore, the words in the Bible are in a language that we do not even speak. Potential misunderstandings and ambiguities lurk at every turn. How can the biblical author possibly communicate in these circumstances? Who is going to arbitrate in the midst of all the interpretive possibilities? Is no one or nothing going to come to the aid of the person who wants to understand the Bible?

The interpreter does have an ally—and a powerful one at that. That indispensable ally is the biblical author himself, and the tool with which he works this magic is the *context*. Yes, there are potential problems and ambiguities in language, but communication works; we do it every day. The word *rock* may be ambiguous, but in the sentence "I threw a rock while listening to rock," you probably know just what I mean (although you may question both my habits and my taste in music). An author controls the expectations of his readers by the way he puts his words together. Context is that indispensable ally that allows a reader to move from what an author's words *might* mean to what he *intended* them to mean. Among all the tools that make communication possible, context is king.

Context is a creation of the author. In fact, that is what makes it so powerful. Any author inherits his language and culture; he does not create them. But the particular way he puts his words together is his to control. In creating a context for his words he is actively working to make the words communicate the right meaning. Context makes communication a mutual process: the author pushes while the reader pulls. At least, this is true of the kind of context I am discussing here. There are other legitimate uses of the word *context* that do refer to things outside the author's control: the historical context, the theological context, and so forth. There is nothing wrong with using *context* in this way, but that is not my topic. I am talking about the written context the author creates, the whole verbal structure within which any part must be understood.

Nothing is more important to the interpreter than the skill of reading in context. This skill lies at the heart of good reading itself. The structure of an author's words gives us access to the structure of his thoughts. No amount of training in Greek and Hebrew, no expertise in ancient history, can make up for an inability to read contextually. If I could be taught by only one person for the rest of my life, I would much rather be taught by a good reader with no training in biblical languages and culture than by a poor reader with years of training. My purpose in this chapter is to demonstrate why.

CONTEXT AND COHERENCE IN HUMAN COMMUNICATION

ANY TEXT MUST be read contextually and coherently if the author is to be understood. In this section I will discuss in simple terms what this means and why it is so. Afterward, we will be in a better position to look at the implications for Bible study.

Context as a Tool for Author and Reader

Although an author may not be consciously aware of it, he is in a battle with ambiguity: words can mean too many things. An author must provide something, sometimes only a few words, to help his reader eliminate the wrong meanings and choose the right one:

- "I prefer fall and spring."
- "She would fall and spring right up again."

Both the word *fall* and the word *spring* are ambiguous. And yet you, the reader, probably understand what I mean by them in these two sentences. How did I, the author, get you to understand? I used your knowledge of English grammar— the first sentence requires *fall* and *spring* to be nouns, but the second sentence needs verbs. I also made your mind search for a way to understand *fall* and *spring* such that they made sense when connected with the word *and*. You did not understand the word *spring* to mean "a bouncy, coiled piece of metal" because in neither sentence would this meaning make sense when paired with the word *fall*.

Now consider the next two sentences:

- "She could not put her watch together again, because she could not find the little spring."
- "She had to go thirsty all day because she could not find the little spring."

The grammar does not help much here, because the word *spring* is in an identical clause in each sentence. Still, I will bet you know what I mean. I am relying on your unquenchable thirst for *what makes sense*. In the first sentence "the little spring" is something that would interfere with putting a watch together if one lost it. Because most of us know that watches have (or, anyway, used to have) little bouncy, coiled pieces of metal inside, this meaning makes the most sense. Likewise, the second sentence requires "the little spring" to be something that would leave someone thirsty if she could not find it. Because all but one of the meanings of *spring* could not even get our heroine wet, much less quench her thirst, I (the author) must mean "water that gushes up from the ground."

Actually, though, that is not what I meant at all. You see, I am afraid I have misled you a little bit. I left off the sentence that came before that second sentence:

- "Although her invention that turned seawater into freshwater was finished, she could not use it because she had lost a small part. She had to go thirsty all day because she could not find the little spring."

This is exactly the same sentence I used in the previous example. In this example, however, the sentence that precedes the "spring" sentence sent your expectations running in a different direction. Before you ever read the "spring" sentence, you knew that a small piece of a machine was missing and were therefore prepared to understand *spring* to mean "a bouncy coil of metal." Further, you were given a reason why losing this piece of metal could make someone go thirsty. This is how context always works. Context molds the expectations of the reader. That can happen in the sentence you are currently reading, anywhere before that sentence, or even after it. The whole of what the author says, from first to last, can provide information that informs the meaning of any one part of it. Finding how the parts relate to the whole, and the whole to the parts, must be the goal of every interpreter.

Context and the Search for Coherence

Consider this excerpt from my soon-to-be-published autobiography: "I do not trust my brother-in-law. Any accountant who owns three yachts and a mansion on the Riviera must be doing something shady." What I mean by these two sentences is so apparent that you might not have noticed that I never actually said that my brother-in-law owns three yachts and a mansion, or even that he is an accountant. But why would I have put those two sentences together if he does not and is not? There is nothing ambiguous about the first or second sentence by itself, but it is not enough to interpret each separately. I, the author, have invited you to make the connection between my untrustworthy brother-in-law and a wealthy accountant; I am the one who knows the whole picture, and I have logically related my sentences so they work together to communicate that whole picture. If you ignore the logical relationship between my sentences when you interpret my words, you will be like someone who picks up a beaded necklace but leaves behind the string—all you will have left is a handful of disconnected pieces. The string that you must not leave behind is the *coherence*.

Implicit in everything I have said so far is the idea that there is some logical relationship among the words, sentences, and paragraphs that an author uses. Is that really true? Is it always true? What is it that gives the structure to these pieces of language scattered throughout the text? The answer to these questions can be found if we consider another of the limitations of words. Not only can words be ambiguous but in addition each word by itself says so little. Think about the words that make up this chapter. Each word is only a piece of what I am trying to say. And what is worse, I can express my thought only one word at a time. In my head I may have a multifaceted and complex idea I am trying to communicate, but I am forced to express it piecemeal, one word after another to form sentences, one sentence after another to form paragraphs, one paragraph after another to form my complete idea. No matter how much I would like to, I cannot give you the whole picture all at once. I have to trust you, the reader, to take the little pieces I give you and put them together. Even though I must be content to express my ideas a word at a time, a sentence at a time, you would be foolish to treat my words and sentences as if they were islands unto themselves. Each sentence that I write forms just a part of the whole idea that I am trying to express; therefore, each sentence is related to the sentences around it. In a word, the text is *coherent.* If you, the reader, will not look for the coherent relationship among my words, sentences, and paragraphs, I'm sunk.

People do speak and write coherently; they do not communicate with each other in fragmented, disjointed words and sentences that bear no relation to each other. Now you may object, "I know that's not true. You haven't read my letters!" True, some of us were the despair of our English teachers as they tried to teach us to present our thoughts in an orderly way. But that is not the point. We may be unskilled at showing the connections among our words, sentences, and paragraphs, but that does not mean there is not a connection in our minds. Only the drugged and the insane speak in sentences that truly do not relate. People speak with a purpose, and that purpose gives coherence to the words they use. And although we may not be conscious of it, we search for that coherence every time we read a book or listen to someone speak. If we did not do this, communication would hardly be possible.

What we must determine to do, in spite of all the pressures of time and all our eagerness (and impatience) to "get to the good stuff," is to follow the author's lead. The author put all those words there for a reason; it is the interpreter's job to figure out what that reason was. There is an inherent logic to every text; the reader must find that logic for the text to communicate. I do not mean to suggest that every text contains only tightly reasoned, logical arguments. Far from it. The book of Proverbs, for example, is a loosely related collection of wise sayings, all of them sharing two characteristics: (1) they are sayings, and (2) they are wise. The "logic" of proverbs is the logic of the list. The author told us so by the way he put the book together. On the other hand, Paul made it pretty clear in Romans that he was presenting logical arguments, drawing conclusions, and bringing out implications; the reader had better pay close attention from beginning to end, because it all hangs together. If I were to read Romans the way I read Proverbs, I would miss most of what is important.

The objection is sometimes raised that this is reading too much into the text. We must do exegesis (drawing our interpretation from the text) and not eisegesis (reading our interpretation into the text). I appreciate the spirit behind this objection. Our goal must be to bring out of the text only the meaning the author put there. If we "read in" more than he meant, then we are just listening to the sound of our own voices. But there is a sense in which we must "read into" a text more than the explicit statements the author made; we must do it because the author expected us to. If someone says to me, "Excuse me, you are standing on my foot," it would be dense of me to keep standing there just because he did not explicitly say, "Please move your foot."

CONTEXT AND COHERENCE AT WORK

THE BEST WAY to understand the role of context is to look at some examples, and that is what we are going to do. In what follows we will look briefly at several passages from the Bible. In each case we will be looking for the interpretation of a word, verse, and so forth that is most coherent. Because this is not a commentary, this is not the place to give elaborate explanations and defenses of my interpretations, and I will not. My goal is to paint pictures of what I think a coherent interpretation looks like and why we must search until we find it. In this format I cannot hope to convince, but I do hope to intrigue.

Context Study: 1 Corinthians 3:10-15

Often we go to a particular passage because it has a reputation as one of *the* passages on a particular subject. This motivation is not necessarily wrong, but it is fraught with interpretive dangers. One danger (among others) is that we are likely to arrive at the passage thinking we already know what it means. For example, if we go to a certain passage because we are interested in spiritual gifts, we tend to ignore the surrounding material that (we think) does not deal directly with spiritual gifts. In doing this we distort the message of the passage. The author never intended one section to be read in isolation. An excellent example of the danger of ignoring context is the interpretation that is often given to 1 Corinthians 3:10-15:

> According to the grace of God which was given to me, like a wise master builder I laid a foundation, and another is building on it. But each man must be careful how he builds on it. For no man can lay a foundation other than the one which is laid, which is Jesus Christ. Now if any man builds on the foundation with gold, silver, precious stones, wood, hay, straw, each man's work will become evident; for the day will show it, because it is to be revealed with fire, and the fire itself will test the quality of each man's work. If any man's work which he has built on it remains, he will receive a reward. If any man's work is burned up, he will suffer loss; but he himself will be saved, yet so as through fire.

This is one of *the* passages concerning the doctrine of rewards. Many times I have heard teachers say that this passage teaches that the quality of my heavenly rewards depends on the quality of my earthly work. I am saved by grace through faith, but rewards come on the basis of my good works that I build on the foundation of my faith in Christ (with suggestions varying as to what the nature of those works might be). This interpretation, however, does not explain how the passage fits into the surrounding context. In fact, I think the surrounding context shows this interpretation to be highly unlikely. Whatever one might think of the doctrine that each believer will receive rewards for his good works on earth, this passage does not support it.

In the case of this passage there are two aspects of the context to be considered: the immediate context and the larger context of chapters 1–4. I want to look briefly at the larger context before we get into the details. Is there any continuity, any overarching theme in these first chapters of 1 Corinthians? Sometimes it is helpful to note the repetition of words, phrases, and ideas. Keeping 1 Corinthians 3:10-15 in mind, consider these verses scattered throughout the first four chapters of 1 Corinthians:

> Now I exhort you, brethren, by the name of our Lord
> Jesus Christ, *that you all agree and that there be no
> divisions among you,* but that you be made complete
> in the same mind and in the same judgment. For I
> have been informed concerning you, my brethren, by
> Chloe's people, *that there are quarrels among you.*
> Now I mean this, that each one of you is saying, *"I
> am of Paul,"* and *"I of Apollos,"* and *"I of Cephas,"* and
> *"I of Christ."* (1 Corinthians 1:10-12, emphasis added)

> Since *there is jealousy and strife among you,* are you
> not fleshly, and are you not walking like mere men?

For when one says, *"I am of Paul,"* and another, *"I am of Apollos,"* are you not mere men? What then is *Apollos?* And what is *Paul?* Servants through whom you believed, even as the Lord gave opportunity to each one. I *[Paul]* planted, *Apollos* watered, but God was causing the growth. So then neither the one who plants nor the one who waters is anything, but God who causes the growth. Now he who plants and he who waters are one; but each will receive his own reward according to his own labor. For we are God's fellow workers; you are God's field, God's building. (1 Corinthians 3:3-9, emphasis added)

Let no one boast in men. For all things belong to you, whether *Paul or Apollos or Cephas* or the world or life or death or things present or things to come; all things belong to you, and you belong to Christ; and Christ belongs to God. (1 Corinthians 3:21-23, emphasis added)

These things, brethren, I have figuratively applied to myself *[Paul]* and *Apollos* for your sakes, so that in us you may learn not to exceed what is written, so that no one of you will *become arrogant in behalf of one against the other.* (1 Corinthians 4:6, emphasis added)

These verses ought to bring joy to any interpreter's heart—the joy of the hound that has caught that first scent of its elusive quarry, the secret satisfaction that brings a gleam to the eye of Sherlock Holmes as he looks up from examining the muddy footprint on the windowsill. In chapter 1 Paul addressed the factionalism that had led the Corinthians to choose sides between himself and Apollos and others, and in chapter 4 he was still talking about it! These verses hold the promise of providing the thread that ties the pieces together into a coherent whole.

Paul's concern was not merely that the Corinthians were not getting along, although he did not like that either. No, what really seems to have been worrying him was *why* they were not getting along. They had chosen up sides concerning their teachers. Some had taken Paul's part, but many saw Apollos as a superior teacher and saw themselves as his disciples. Such factionalism is bad; after all, we are all disciples of Christ. But what defect in their hearts and minds had led them to dismiss the apostle Paul as an inferior teacher? Seemingly, they had embraced a worldly (and presumably Greek) notion of "wisdom" by which they judged their teachers. Apollos seemed to qualify; Paul did not. But this was terrible. Paul's straightforward proclamation of the gospel, the message of life, was being dismissed by the Corinthians as not quite good enough. Everything Paul wrote in this section was meant to address this perverse worldliness on the part of the Corinthians. This is why he dismissed the wisdom of the world and extolled the wisdom of the Cross. This is why he explained to the Corinthians that he deliberately relied on the power of the gospel message instead of persuasive oratory when he first came to teach them. This is why he defended his gospel as true wisdom that he received directly from the Spirit of God Himself. And this is why, in the passage we are looking at, he talked about wood, hay, and stubble.

Now let us turn to the immediate context. Just before our passage, Paul was explaining the perspective the Corinthians ought to have been taking toward him and Apollos. The worldliness in Corinth had led to misperceptions of these two men who so greatly influenced the church. Paul set out to correct those perceptions. He used two metaphors: (1) Paul and Apollos were *workers* in God's *field,* the Corinthian church; and (2) Paul and Apollos were *builders* of God's *building,* the Corinthian church. Notice that I am saying that

Paul and Apollos, not Christians in general, were the builders. I think this becomes clear when we see that the foundation metaphor is not standing by itself but is a restatement of the field metaphor just before it. Notice the crucial verse 9, where Paul switched from the field metaphor to the building metaphor. This verse not only ties verses 5 through 9 together with verses 10 through 15; it also ties the two metaphors intimately together. When we see how the two are tied together, we can also see that they are parallel to each other. Below is a chart that describes how the two metaphors relate to the reality of the situation in Corinth:

The Reality	First Metaphor	Second Metaphor
God was at work in the Corinthian Church.	The Corinthian church was God's field.	The Corinthian church was God's building.
Paul and Apollos were merely servants of God to the Corinthians.	Paul and Apollos were workers in God's field.	Paul and Apollos were builders of God's building.
Paul preached Christ to the Corinthians first, founded the church, and then left.	Paul planted.	Paul laid the foundation (which is Christ) as a wise master builder.
Apollos came and taught the Corinthians after Paul left.	Apollos watered.	Another was building upon it.
Paul and Apollos were each responsible before God for what they taught the Corinthians.	He who planted and he who watered were one, but each would receive his own reward according to his own labor.	Let each man be careful how he built upon it.

The interpretation that sees the doctrine of a believer's rewards for good works in this passage has pulled Paul's metaphor out of the context where he explained what it means. It is easy to understand how this might happen. Once we start thinking of 1 Corinthians 3:10-15 as "the place where Paul talks about rewards," our attention is drawn to those verses, and we have no particular motivation to think very long about the verses that describe Paul and Apollos and the Corinthians (after all, they have all been dead a long time). The context, however, shows us that the issue Paul addressed is not how one lives one's life as a Christian but rather how Apollos and others continued Paul's work in teaching the Corinthians. The chart below compares what I see as the wrong way and the right way to understand the building metaphor in 1 Corinthians 3:10-15:

The Metaphor	Does Not Mean	Does Mean
A builder	Each believer	Apollos and others
of a building	in his own life	in the Corinthian church
builds on a foundation	builds on his faith	builds on Paul's teachings
with precious stones	with good works	with good teaching
or with worthless stuff.	or with evil works.	or with false teaching.

There are still questions (which I will not go into here) that we need to answer about the passage. Chief among them, perhaps, is the nature of the "reward" or "wage" that the workers Paul and Apollos could expect for their labors. But if our goal in interpreting 1 Corinthians 3:10-15 is a coherent interpretation, one that puts all the pieces of Paul's argument together the way he intended, then our inevitable starting place must be this: to understand the building metaphor in just the way Paul intended. And *that* we can do only by noting how Paul sets up the metaphor in the verses that precede it.

Context Study: 2 Corinthians 3:1-6

Pronouns are prime examples of words that must be understood in context. Who is "he"? What is "it"? Without a context, it is impossible to know. Our next example has an ambiguous pronoun that we must successfully pin down: "Not that we are adequate in ourselves to consider anything as coming from ourselves, but our adequacy is from God, who also made us adequate as servants of a new covenant" (2 Corinthians 3:5-6). The pronoun *we* sometimes gives us trouble. Out of an appropriate desire to apply the biblical statements to our own lives, we sometimes take the shortcut of assuming that *we* means "all of us Christians." The statement is then immediately relevant to each and every one of us. We must resist this temptation. We need to take particular care to let an author's pronouns point at whom or what he chooses. To be specific, who is the "we" in "not that we are adequate"? Was Paul talking about Christians in general or someone else?

The first temptation we must resist is to answer this question theologically. Does the adequacy of every Christian come from God? Of course it does. Of course we are inadequate in ourselves. Of course we want God to make us adequate. But while we are busy preaching ourselves that sermon, Scripture may be trying to preach another. At this point we are not asking whether our interpretation fits our theology; we are asking whether our interpretation fits the words Paul used.

Paul seems to have always had a stormy relationship with the Corinthians. In the first and second chapters of 2 Corinthians, Paul found it necessary to recount his recent travels. Actually, he had to defend his recent travels, for some Corinthians seem to have been put out at his change of plans—he did not visit them the way he said he would. This had put him in a position of having to defend his motives and his ministry to them. In the last verse of chapter 2 he said, "We are not like many, peddling the word of God, but as from sincerity, but as from God, we speak in Christ in the sight of God" (2:17). The

Corinthians often put Paul in the position of having to speak up for himself. But this was a difficult spot for Paul to be in. On the one hand, he was an apostle of Jesus Christ. On the other hand, he was just a man. It would be inappropriate to brag, yet it would also be inappropriate to let the Corinthians look down on a representative of Christ. So he said, "Are we beginning to commend ourselves again? Or do we need, as some, letters of commendation to you or from you?" (3:1). Paul was saying to them, "Look, don't you know me well enough that I should not have to say these things? We are not just starting out in our relationship. I do not need to bring a letter of reference to prove my apostolic credentials." Notice particularly who "we" and "you" are: Paul spoke of himself as "we" and the Corinthians as "you." We should not be surprised that Paul spoke of himself in the plural; he did it all the time. There are various explanations given for this: that he was using the "royal *we*" or "editorial *we*"; that he was including Timothy (who is listed as cowriter of this letter); that he was including the rest of the apostles. Here, though, he can clearly only have meant himself. Note the pronouns in the next section:

> *You* are *our* letter, written in *our* hearts, known and
> read by all men; being manifested that *you* are a let-
> ter of Christ, cared for by *us,* written not with ink
> but with the Spirit of the living God, not on tablets
> of stone but on tablets of human hearts. (3:2-3,
> emphasis added)

In other words, Paul was saying, "I already have a letter of recommendation: it is you. All you or anyone would have to do to evaluate my ministry is to look at what has happened in your midst." Paul built on the metaphor of the letter. This letter was a letter of Christ, which had been ministered by Paul. Notice the thin line Paul was walking here. On the one hand, he was defending his own ministry; this "letter" was "cared for

114 | The Language of God

by us." On the other hand, *Paul* was not the one who had worked the changes in their hearts; that was the work of Christ through His Spirit. Paul was the servant of a powerful Master. Also, we should note that Paul was talking about the specific work of Paul and the Spirit in the lives of the Corinthians. This was not an abstract dissertation on the Christian life.

He continued: "Such confidence *we* have through Christ toward God" (3:4, emphasis added). Who is "we" in this verse? The most natural way to understand this "we" is to assume it is the same "we" it has been all along: Paul. This fits with the language of "such confidence." The word "such" points back to what he had just been talking about. He had been claiming that the Corinthians were evidence of the power of his ministry, that his ministry had led to the Spirit of God writing on the tablets of their hearts. He recognized that this was a big claim—the claim that one man could have such a powerful ministry. He *was* confident this was true, but his confidence was based in Christ, not in himself.

He went on to spell this out in our problem verses: "Not that we are adequate in ourselves to consider anything as coming from ourselves, but our adequacy is from God, who also made us adequate as servants of a new covenant" (3:5-6). The same "we" has carried all the way through. Paul was saying that he himself was not adequate to account for the tremendous impact his ministry had had. But God had made him an adequate minister of the new covenant. In fact, he was going to go on to extol the new covenant itself as the reason his ministry was so powerful. Clearly the adequacy being discussed was not the adequacy of every Christian but Paul's own adequacy. I would paraphrase this section as follows:

> I have no need to commend myself to you Corinthians; you yourselves are the best defense my ministry could have. My ministry has led to a change among you that can be seen by all. I speak with the confi-

dence of a totally adequate minister of the gospel,
not because I think I am capable of such things on
my own but because God has made me what I
never could have made myself.

Does this distinction make a difference in what we learn
from this passage? I think it does. We Christians clearly need
to rely on God for our adequacy, but the question is this: for
what tasks has God promised to make us adequate? Paul was
talking about what God did to make him a minister of the
gospel, that is, an apostle. Paul's adequacy as a minister of the
gospel was of an entirely different order than mine or yours
or Billy Graham's. Paul was defending his unchallengeable
authority to a people who were all too ready to challenge it
loudly and often. This passage does not tell us that God has
promised to supernaturally empower our ministry (although
that could very well be true). Rather, it tells us that we can put
total confidence in what Paul taught, because God had supernaturally empowered *his* ministry. We will have to look to other
passages to pin down what God has promised to do for *us*.
The context has put strong demands on the "we" in this passage; therefore, however attractive the other interpretation
might be initially, it must ultimately be rejected as not fitting the
surrounding context.

Context Study: 1 Corinthians 11:10

For this next example I am not going to propose an interpretation. However, some of the debate that has raged around this
verse is quite instructive. It brings us face to face with the issue
of just how far we should let context take us. This is the verse
under consideration, as translated by the New American Standard Bible: "The woman ought to have a symbol of authority
on her head, because of the angels" (1 Corinthians 11:10). The
translators have made an interpretive decision here and added
some words to make clear what they think Paul was saying.

More literally, the Greek says, "The woman ought to have authority over her head [or 'on her head'], because of the angels."

For a long time the standard interpretation of this verse has been that Paul was telling women to wear head coverings as a sign of their husbands' authority. In modern times, however, this interpretation has been challenged. The argument against the standard interpretation is a simple one: the Greek doesn't say, "Have a symbol of authority"; it says, "Have authority." According to this line of argument, the meaning of the Greek is simple, clear, and unambiguous. Paul said that women ought to have authority over their heads. Period. To suggest anything else is to ignore the plain meaning of the Greek and put words in Paul's mouth.

I want to respond to this argument because of the important interpretive issue that it raises. This argument implies that the meaning of the Greek in this verse is obvious and self-evident. But that is a naïve view of language that ignores the role of context in determining meaning. There is a dynamic relationship, a kind of tug of war that happens between context and word meaning. Language convention does not control the meaning of a text; the author does. Otherwise, an author could never use words in a unique way. Remember what I said at the beginning: context is king.

I have made up a story to show you what I mean:

> Linda enters the classroom to take an important test. The teacher has left a list of do's and dont's for each student to consult. Linda reads the list and then says to Manuel, "It says here that we are supposed to fill out our test forms at one of the tables in the middle of the room. But I may need to consult the reference book that is on the table in the corner. I don't care what the rules say; I'm going to do it by the book."

The phrase "doing it by the book" usually means "following

the rules." But in this context things have changed. First of all, it is clear that the speaker is *not* going to follow the rules, so she cannot be saying that. Furthermore, she is discussing the location where she is going to do something, so "by the book" in this case must mean "next to the book." Although the phrase "doing it by the book" conventionally means "following the rules," that convention is not strong enough to override the context.

How far can an author go? Can he take a word and make it mean something it clearly does not mean? Ask the first person who said something was "bad" when he meant it was good. Ask your local sports announcer, the one who yells, "Yessir, folks, he swatted that tangerine right over the left field fence." Tangerine? *Tangerine* does not mean "baseball." The announcer in this case, however, thought that he had such a strong context that no one could possibly misunderstand him. And of course, he was right. If he had said "refrigerator," we would ask him after the game, "Why did you call the baseball a refrigerator?" We might think it was a stupid thing to say, but *we would not misunderstand.* Context is that powerful.

I am not going to make a case for any particular interpretation of 1 Corinthians 11:10, but I do want to come to the defense of those who see "a sign of authority" in Paul's language. They have not imposed some foreign idea on the text. They have not willfully ignored the Greek construction in the passage. They have made their best attempt at putting the context and the language conventions together in a way that makes sense. First of all, this line of interpretation sees the basic message of the passage as "men should not pray with a head covering, but women should." Now look at the language that precedes our verse (verses 7-9, parentheses mine):

A man ought not to have his head covered, since he is the image and glory of God; but the woman is the glory of man. (For man does not originate from

woman, but woman from man; for indeed man was
not created for the woman's sake, but woman for
the man's sake.)

I put parentheses around verses 8 and 9 to indicate that they
are just explanatory material; they explain more about why
woman is the glory of man. If, for the sake of seeing more
clearly the structure of Paul's main argument, we remove the
explanatory material, it looks like this (emphasis added):

A man *ought not to have his head covered,* since he
is the image and glory of God; but the woman is the
glory of man. . . . Therefore the woman *ought to
have* authority *on her head.*

We see two "mirror image" arguments, one for the man and
one for the woman. We could picture it like this:

A   A man ought not to have his head covered,
B   since he is the image and glory of God;
B' but the woman is the glory of man.
A' Therefore the woman ought to have [something] on
her head.

The case for "a sign of authority" rests on the assumption that
this is the structure of Paul's argument. And we must acknowledge that this is a reasonable and natural way to take it. Yes,
it is true that "to have authority over" is an expression that
occurs in Greek. But the structure of the argument leads us to
expect Paul to say something about headgear. The man "ought
not have his head covered," but the woman "ought to have
[something] on her head." Given this reading of the context, we
expect that the "something" represents a head covering. Now
the difficult decisions start. The "something" that Paul says she
ought to have on her head is "authority." This is an unusual use

of the word. We need to recognize that. We are caught in the classic tug of war. The meaning of "authority" seems to be pulling in one direction; the context seems to be pulling in another. What are we going to do?

The context must win; that is how language works. I am not saying our work is done on this passage. Far from it. We need to examine the evidence concerning "authority" carefully, to see just how unusual this usage is. We need to examine the context to see if there is another, even more compelling reading. Maybe the structure of the argument is not the way I have presented it. But if we cannot find that compelling alternative, then we must let the standard interpretation stand. I am not concerned here with authority or head coverings. I am concerned with interpretive methods. It is not wrong for an interpreter to let a strong context suggest an unusual meaning for a word. If we do not do this, then context has lost its power to control our understanding, and the author has lost his power to communicate.

Context Study: James 5:13-15

We are finally ready to resolve the questions we have raised concerning James 5:13-15. We have waited to do so until this chapter on context and coherence for a reason: context is the author's tool for getting past the ambiguities of language, including the kinds of ambiguities we find in this passage. As we have seen in a previous chapter, two different Greek words (astheneō and kamnō) are usually translated "sick" in James 5:13-15. We also saw that neither of these words necessarily mean "sick"; one is just as often translated "weak" and the other "weary." Now this fact alone does not mean that the translators were wrong when they translated them both as "sick" nor that the common interpretation of James 5 (that it is describing how to be healed from sickness) is wrong. The results of our word study have raised a question, not settled it. But a question has indeed been raised: do the proponents of the common interpretation of this passage have good reason for rejecting "weak" and "weary" and choosing "sick" as the correct understanding of the Greek words? Probably many of us would not have realized that such a question needed to be answered, because all the translators whose works we use chose "sick" as the appropriate translation—*without telling us that they made that decision for us.* This is not an indictment of translations; every translator has to make interpretive decisions. Nevertheless, we need to recognize that the word *sick* in our English Bibles is an interpretive decision by the translators, one that must be defended. Which translation of these words ("sick" or "weak/weary") best fits the context? Which understanding of James 5:13-15 is most coherent?

"These are the times that try men's souls" is a line that could have come from James instead of Thomas Paine. In such times a person discovers the reality (or lack of it) behind his religious sentiments. James' readers faced great social and economic pressures that brought them face to face with one of life's fundamental questions: what does my faith really mean to me? Into this situation James spoke both a message of encouragement and a message of warning. The warning is a stern one, stern enough to give the letter the dark tone that makes so many Christians nervous when they read it. James told his original readers how a real trust in God leaves a mark in a believer's life, and he warned them that the way they had responded to their trials showed no evidence of that mark. James feared for his audience. He saw them compromising their faith to such an extent that he was afraid they had no faith at all. *Saying* we trust God is not faith; *trusting* God is faith. This was James' message, for instance, in the infamous "faith and works" section in chapter 2.

But James also sounded another note in his letter—a note of encouragement and redemption. In a situation where the great temptation was to envy and emulate the wealthy men who were plaguing them, James reminded his readers where the true riches lie. James 1:12 sums up his message well: "Blessed is a man who perseveres under trial; for once he has been approved, he will receive the crown of life which the Lord has promised to those who love Him." If James' readers really believed the promises God had made, then the implications were clear: the poor exploited believer is richer than the richest man on earth. James also recognized, however, that his encouragement might revive the waning resolve of believers who had been living foolish, self-centered, and worldly lives. Thus there is a redemptive strain in James' words as well. God grants wisdom "without reproach" (James 1:5). James told his readers, "Draw near to God and He will draw near to you" (4:8). As James neared the end of his letter, he made his strongest appeal for his readers to continue in the faith: The prize is worth the wait, he urged; live your lives with the eager and patient expectation that the Lord is coming to restore all things; do not give up the fight; live like the farmer who endures the long days of cultivation because he is eager for the harvest; remember the men of old who persevered in the midst of suffering, and think of what God did for them in the end.

And so James concluded his letter of stern warning and encouragement with some questions and answers (5:13): Are you suffering hardship? Are you facing persecution and temptation and all that I just said you must strengthen your hearts to endure? Do not despair; turn to God in prayer. Are you of good courage? Are you keeping your spirits up in this time of difficulty? Rejoice and thank God. And then James came to one more question: Is anyone among you *asthenei?* And so our questions begin.

I think that the notion of James as the New Testament book of proverbs—a common notion—has dulled our perceptions. We have failed, for the most part, to notice just how anticlimactic and discordant the popular understanding of James 5:13-15 is. James, from his first sentence until the end of his letter, had been urging his readers not to abandon their faith in God, no matter what suffering it might cost them. The issues he had confronted were eternal ones: inheriting the crown of life, entering the kingdom, having a faith that is effective for salvation. "Behold, the Judge is standing right at the door" (James 5:9). Then, according to the popular interpretation, James digressed to discuss how to be supernaturally healed of sickness before he resumed talking about eternal issues again in the last two verses. This seeming incongruity in the passage should cause us to ask if there is another interpretive option that fits the context better. To say the least, as interpreters we ought to be extremely interested in an interpretation of James 5:13-15 that is more relevant to the theme that has dominated the book of James up to this point: suffering under persecution and perseverance in the faith.

At this point the results of our word study become important. We have seen that *astheneō* can mean either "sick" or "weak." That is, it describes a weakness of either the body or of the mind, emotions, and spirit. Which of these does the context lead us to expect? Which follows most coherently from what James just said? To my mind, there is no question: everything James has said prepares me to hear "weak" in this context. It fits the argument of the whole book. It fits the argument of the passage that precedes it (5:7-12): Be patient, strengthen your hearts, suffer hardship, and persevere. But are you weak? It fits with the two other questions with which it is grouped. Are you suffering hardship? Are you of good courage? Or are you weak?

How about our other ambiguous word, *kamnō* (James 5:15)? Let me remind you of the only other place where it occurs in the New Testament, Hebrews 12:1-3:

> Since we have so great a cloud of witnesses surrounding us, let us also lay aside every encumbrance and the sin which so easily entangles us, and let us run with endurance the race that is set before

us, fixing our eyes on Jesus, the author and perfecter
of faith, who for the joy set before Him endured the
cross, despising the shame, and has sat down at the
right hand of the throne of God.

For consider Him who has endured such hostility
by sinners against Himself, so that you will not *grow
weary* and lose heart. (emphasis added)

In this passage to "grow weary" is the opposite of "endurance"
in faith. This has got to make us sit up and take notice. The
situation the author addressed in Hebrews corresponds exactly
to the situation James discussed throughout his book. The
author of the Hebrews passage encouraged believers not to
grow weary in the face of opposition and distress, to persevere
in faith. But to face such difficulty can cause us to flag in our
perseverance; it can make us grow weary. This is exactly what
James was warning his readers against. The one who is "weary"
in the struggle to persevere in the faith needs to seek the support of others in prayer. The one who is "weak" in faith in the
face of hardship needs to lean on those whose faith is strong.
Here is my translation of James 5:13-15:

Is anyone among you suffering hardship? Let him
pray. Is anyone of good courage? Let him sing
praises. Is anyone among you weak? Let him call for
the elders of the church, and let them pray over
him, anointing him with oil in the name of the Lord;
and the prayer offered in faith will save the one who
is weary, and the Lord will raise him up, and if he
has committed sins, they will be forgiven him.

James 5:13-15 by itself, apart from the larger context, is
truly ambiguous. It is far from stupid for someone to have
decided that James was referring to sickness. What concerns
the authors of this book, however, is the almost total ignoring

of the other interpretive possibility in the standard literature on James. How much more convincing the "sickness" interpretation would be if it had won in a fair fight, that is, if it could be demonstrated that it better fits the context. (At this point, however, we do not think this could be demonstrated.) Ultimately our argument for James 5:13-15 depends on our understanding of the content of James' letter that precedes these verses. To our minds, the "weak and weary" interpretation provides a much more powerful, appropriate, and *coherent* conclusion to the book of James—the best argument that can be made for the correctness of any interpretation.

CONCLUSION

THE ROLE OF context in interpretation is radical and fundamental. We in the modern church do partly understand the dangers of interpreting "out of context." We have learned through bitter experience that it is dangerous to pull verses out of context, and we have very rightly encouraged each other not to do so. Cults often do this very thing, taking verses out of context and building distinctive and quirky doctrines on the shaky platform those verses provide. Most of us have seen similar kinds of things, and we know full well we should not do it.

What we acknowledge in theory, however, we have not always done in practice. Many of us still view the Bible with a "proverbs mentality," a mental image of the Bible as a collection of wise sayings. We so want the Bible to speak to our situation in life that we become impatient; we forget that the great wisdom in the Bible comes in the form of letters and histories and poetry. We still tend to pull individual verses out and apply them before we have grounded our understanding of the verse in the surrounding context. We have to fight this tendency. We must not allow ourselves to settle for anything less than a coherent understanding of the passage.

There are really no magic techniques for developing solid,

coherent interpretations. All it takes is the ability to read. Now, when I say this, I do not mean to suggest that it is easy. The sad fact is that in our culture the ability to read with understanding is a vanishing art. We must relearn what we already know. When we learned to read, some potent tools were put into our hands, but for many of us they have grown rusty with disuse. If we seriously want to become good, principled interpreters of the Bible, we must start using those tools again. We must read often. We must think about what we read and talk about what we read and then read and think about it again. We must not be hasty and we must not be stubborn; we must let the biblical author tell his own story. Only then can we be confident that the biblical message has changed us and not the other way around.

STUDY QUESTIONS[1]

1. Prepare a response to the following statement:

> There is more than one way in which we know the will of God. But according to Colossians 3:15, one important way we can know His will is through the peace of Christ ruling in our hearts. If chaos rules in our hearts over some decision, then it is not God's will. But if the peace of Christ rules in our hearts over that decision, we can know that we are in His will.

2. Prepare a response to the following statement:

> Smoking, drinking, and abusing drugs are not specifically prohibited in the Scriptures, yet they are clearly in violation of Scripture. First Corinthians 6:19 tells us that we are a temple of the Holy Spirit. First Corinthians

3:17 further tells us that anyone who destroys his body (the temple of God) will himself be destroyed by God. Because smoking, drinking, and drug taking are activities that are harmful to our bodies, they are activities in which Christians ought not take part.

3. Prepare a response to the following statement:

According to Galatians 3:28, we are all one in Christ. Among believers, no barriers or distinctions can rightfully exist. We are equal in every respect. There should therefore be no social distinctions allowed among us. But all too often even we Christians distinguish between men and women in the rights and privileges we allow men over women. According to Galatians 3:28, this ought not be so.

CHAPTER FIVE

Background Information

"Thank you, it's a very interesting dance to watch," said Alice, feeling very glad that it was over at last: "and I do so like that curious song about the whiting!"

"Oh, as to the whiting," said the Mock Turtle, "they— you've seen them, of course?"

"Yes," said Alice, "I've often seen them at dinn—" she checked herself hastily.

"I don't know where Dinn may be," said the Mock Turtle, "but if you've seen them so often, of course you know what they're like."

"I believe so," Alice replied thoughtfully. "They have their tails in their mouths—and they're all over crumbs."

"You're wrong about the crumbs," said the Mock Turtle: "crumbs would all wash off in the sea. But they *have* their tails in their mouths, and the reason is—" here the Mock Turtle yawned and shut his eyes—"Tell her about the reason and all that," he said to the Gryphon.

"The reason is," said the Gryphon, "that they *would* go with the lobsters to the dance. So they got thrown out to sea. So they had to fall a long way. So they got their tails fast in their mouths. So they couldn't get them out again. That's all."

"Thank you," said Alice, "it's very interesting. I never knew so much about a whiting before."

I LEARNED MY FIRST lesson about background information a long time ago, when I was not yet a Christian. I was just out of high school and engaged in that battle with God that was to result in my becoming a believer. Like many people who have waged that war before me, I was desperately searching for ammunition to use against my Enemy. My attitude was much like that of W. C. Fields. When asked what a reprobate like him was doing reading the Bible, Fields is said to have replied, "I'm looking for loopholes." One of my strategies was to go on search-and-destroy missions through the Bible. I was on the lookout for anything dubious that I could use to justify my non-belief. On one of my forays I caught the apostle Paul using an obviously savage and grisly metaphor: "If your enemy is hungry, feed him, and if he is thirsty, give him a drink; for in so doing you will heap burning coals on his head" (Romans 12:20, quoting Proverbs 25:21-22). *Aha!* I rejoiced inwardly. *Is this barbarian the one to teach morality and ethics to me?* (You will have noticed that I was being totally unfair to Paul, but be patient with me; I was young and desperate.) I pointed this out to a Christian who used to listen patiently to my ranting, and he gave me an intriguing reply. The reason this verse sounded wrong to me, he said, was because I was missing some important information about the background. In those days people used to carry the hot coals they needed for cooking in a container on their heads. Heaping burning coals on someone's head was a way of giving them the necessities of life.

Now this was staggering news—not that people carried coals in buckets on their heads, but that such a simple piece of information could cause such a complete turnaround of meaning. Burning coals had suggested something negative and painful to me, but now I saw that they could mean something positive and healing. You cannot get much more dramatic a change in meaning than from negative to positive. Now, I did not immediately surrender and become a believer; that was still to come. But I did learn my first lesson concerning the importance of background information: *background information can profoundly change our understanding of the author's intent.*

Alas, my new interpretation of the burning coals passage

was soon shot down, giving me my second lesson in background information in the process. To my disappointment, I found that few others agreed with this way of taking Romans 12:20. Most interpreters rejected this argument as unconvincing and unlikely, if they referred to it at all. Many took the burning coals on the head to be a picture of the painful shame and remorse that an enemy would feel when we respond to him with kindness.

Soon I found myself with a number of questions: Did people really carry on their heads hot coals for cooking? Where would I go to find out? Even if they did, is it necessarily relevant for understanding Proverbs and Paul? Must every reference to "burning coals on the head" be taken this way? What about 2 Esdras in the Apocrypha, where it says, "The sinner must not deny that he has sinned; he will only bring burning coals on to his own head if he says, 'I have committed no sin against the majesty of God'"? (16:53, NEB). This clearly does not refer to giving someone the hot coals he needs for cooking! Does not this text in fact suggest that "hot coals on the head" may have been a different kind of metaphor altogether? Does my way of taking the passage even make sense? Give your enemy food and drink because you will give him the hot coals he needs for cooking? Is not "food and drink" already a clearer way of saying "the necessary things of life" than "hot coals on your head" would be?

The more I thought about it, the less I liked my new way of taking Romans 12:20. It was my first lesson in interpretive humility; I had to scrap a favorite interpretation because it did not hold up under scrutiny. But it was also my second lesson in the uses of background information: *background information can be ambiguous and difficult to apply to a passage.*

There is a great wealth of historical knowledge available to us, but such knowledge comes with a blessing and a curse. It holds out the blessing of a fuller understanding of the text, but it threatens us with the curse of befuddlement. A piece of historical information might be used to make sense of an obscure passage. Or that same piece of historical information might be misused to make a truly screwy interpretation sound plausible. An interpreter likes nothing more than to get relevant facts. But are they facts? And are they relevant? And how do we know?

My purpose in this chapter is to bring home the potential blessing and curse of background information. In what follows I first want to *inspire* you with the idea that background studies truly can bear fruit. Next, I want to *sober* you with some warnings about how simplistic background studies can deceive us. Finally, we will look at some more examples from the Bible. My purpose is not to teach biblical history and culture, just as the chapter on language conventions did not teach Greek and Hebrew. Rather, I want to help us think clearly about background information—what it is and how we should use it.

COMMON KNOWLEDGE AND COMMON IGNORANCE

COMMUNICATION REQUIRES COMMON knowledge. If I want to talk to you, I have to assume that you know some of the same things I do, or we will never get anywhere. A number of years ago Pioneer 10 was launched into space with a "message from planet Earth" engraved on the outside. The scientists who "wrote" that message had a big problem: how do you communicate with someone you know absolutely nothing about? Common knowledge comes through common experience; what experiences do we have in common with a protoplasmic blob from Alpha Centauri? The scientists drew a picture of a man and a woman, but they did so without any great hopes that an alien would know what it was looking at, if it even had eyes at all. The scientists decided that science itself might be used as a kind of universal language, so they included a sort of coded drawing based on (presumably) common scientific knowledge. (I must add that if extraterrestrial life ever sends a coded message to us, we had better hope I am not the one who gets it; I could not have deciphered the picture on Pioneer 10 in a million years.) We humans can communicate with each other much more easily. Although we differ in many ways, we are more alike than not. We can assume a great deal about each other, and that is why our attempts at communication are successful so often.

We have already seen this at work in our discussion of language convention. If I expect to understand what an author has written, then I must understand the language he used. I must know its vocabulary and its grammar. The author does not tell me those things; he assumes I know them already. If I do not, communication breaks down. There is more, however, than just the conventions of language that the reader must know. Consider this sentence: "Bob is lying on the floor in front of the fire, scratching his fleas and gnawing on a bone." Your knowledge of English vocabulary tells you what words such as *lying, floor, scratching,* and *fleas* mean. Your knowledge of English grammar tells you that Bob is the one doing the lying, scratching, and gnawing and that the floor, fleas, and bone are the ones being lain on, scratched, and gnawed. But there is more than English language convention at work in this sentence. Don't you, the reader, feel fairly certain that Bob is a dog? (At least, for his sake, let us hope he is a dog.) I did not say he is a dog; I never even used the word *dog.* What put the idea of "dog" in your head? I, the author, was betting that your experience of life has been similar to mine. The picture this sentence paints is one that fits dogs. I have often seen dogs doing this, and I have never seen a human do it. (Nor do I ever want to.) Is that not your experience as well? I believed this sentence would say "dog" to you because I believed that we share the same background information. I did not have to say it, because you already knew it.

As we speak and write, we tailor our words to fit our

mental image of the audience. We start with the assumption that the audience knows roughly what we know, with some exceptions. We bother to explain only the exceptions. When I tell my wife that she should return a friend's phone call, I do not include a detailed explanation of how to dial the telephone. With a young child, however, I would. In his bestseller *Cultural Literacy,* E. D. Hirsch describes modern studies dealing with the role of background information in communication.[1] One study looked at the way people answered a request for subway directions. When the one asking for directions gave the impression that he was a native, people gave short, cryptic answers. When they thought the person was a tourist, however, they gave much more detailed answers. They only provided as much explanation as they thought the person needed to hear.

Unfortunately, the speaker is sometimes wrong about his audience. If I am a tourist but the person I ask for directions thinks I am a native, I may be just as lost after the explanation as I was before. When my children were younger and would listen in when I was talking to my wife, I was not really thinking about them as part of my "audience." Inevitably they would jump in with interpretive questions: "What do you mean?" "Who are you talking about?" "Why did she do that?" When the level of explanation does not match the level of understanding, confusion is likely. And like it or not, this is the problem we modern readers of the Bible face. We are not the audience that the biblical authors had in mind. We are tourists in their world, but they are talking to us like natives. In our knowledge of the biblical world we are children, but they are treating us like adults.

So we have a problem—not insoluble but significant. We do not know everything that the biblical authors expected us, their audience, to know. Actually, it is worse than that: we know different things than the biblical authors expected their audience to know. This is dangerous. It is one thing to lack a piece of information; much worse is to have the wrong information and not know it. How many situation-comedy plots have turned on this? The husband is talking to someone about how he will have to have his dog put to sleep. The wife overhears and, assuming she understands the background behind his words, thinks he is talking about her. From then on, his every word and act is interpreted in the sinister light of this bogus information. The wrong background information can fool us into thinking we understand when we do not.

Think about the background information required to understand the following two verses:

> Every woman who has her head uncovered while praying or prophesying disgraces her head, for she is one and the same as the woman whose head is shaved. (1 Corinthians 11:5)

> "Whatever you have said in the dark will be heard in the light, and what you have whispered in the inner rooms will be proclaimed upon the housetops." (Luke 12:3)

In the 1 Corinthians passage it is not hard to see that there are cultural factors at work that we moderns are missing. To me it sounds like a riddle: why is a woman without a head covering like one with a shaved head? I cannot get Paul's point without knowing the significance for Paul and his readers of a shaved head on a woman. I am ignorant, but at least I know I am ignorant. When I first read this verse, I was not tempted to think I understood it.

Jesus' words in the second verse, however, seem perfectly straightforward. When I first read them, it never even occurred to me that I needed any first-century background information to understand this. What is not to understand? The picture is of a person climbing up on the top of a high rooftop and

shouting out private words to the crowd below, right? I thought
of the neighborhoods I am familiar with, with row upon row
of houses with pitched roofs. I saw a crazy man trying to balance on the point of one of these roofs, crying out, "You should
hear what I just heard." Crowds gather below, crying out, "Look
at that man! He's crazy; he'll break his neck!" The wild-eyed
prophet teeters high above the crowd as he screams out his
message. All of this came to mind for one simple reason: I
thought I knew perfectly well what a "housetop" was.

Jack Crabtree first pointed out to me what houses were
like in Jesus' day. There were inner rooms, which were the
most private; then an outer courtyard; and finally stairs that
went up to the flat roof, which was essentially another room
in the house. (Remember how Peter went up on the housetop to pray in Acts 10.) Everyone went up on their roofs in
the evening to escape the heat that had built up inside the
house and to enjoy the evening breeze. Now what picture do
we get of something "proclaimed upon the housetops"? We
see a man and wife and their guests sitting on the roof in the
cool of the evening and discussing some particularly juicy bit
of news. The news is so interesting that they pass it on to
their neighbors, who are sitting on their respective roofs. Soon
each housetop is abuzz with it. It has come out of the inner
room, which was the most private place a person had, and
found its way to the housetops, which were the most public.
In small-town America we might say, "It will become the talk
of the front porches," which in the evening serve a similar
function to that of Palestinian housetops. All of this I totally
missed because it never occurred to me that a biblical "house"
might be quite different from the ones I know. This is why I
say that having *no* information is less dangerous than having
the *wrong* information.

My problem is not so much that I do not live in the first
century but that I *do* live in the twenty-first century. My head
is overflowing with facts, beliefs, ideas, and experiences, many

of which will mislead me if I read them into the Bible. For this reason, the first step toward interpretive skill is not to buy a Bible encyclopedia but to change my way of thinking. I need to become sensitive to the potential differences between my world and the biblical world. The text is not going to flash a sign at me: Insert Missing Background Info Here. I have to be prepared to exercise my imagination. Most importantly, I need to bring intellectual humility to the text. The background understanding I bring to the text may be the wrong one, and I need to be prepared—even eager—to acknowledge that and correct it. Understanding requires humility; this is true of Bible study as well as anything else.

FIRST CORINTHIANS 1–4 REVISITED

IN THE EARLY chapters of 1 Corinthians, Paul referred in several places to the way the Corinthians had chosen sides between him and Apollos. We discussed this in the previous chapter on context, and we saw that this was potentially a thread that ties the early chapters together. Paul did not merely lament the divisiveness among his original readers. He seemed even more concerned with the thinking and values that led some to favor Apollos over him. Paul did not, however, explain what the relationships among himself, Apollos, and the Corinthians had been. Why should he have? Everyone to whom he was writing had lived through the whole thing. This does, however, make it harder for us to understand Paul's point. What problem did Paul see? How were the Corinthians thinking about Apollos? About Paul? What was Paul's warning?

In such a situation the best source of information, if it has any to give, is the Bible itself. There are two helpful strategies in this case: (1) Use a concordance and look for every reference to Apollos in the Bible. (2) Read both letters to the Corinthians and look for evidence of how things stood between Paul and the Corinthians.

When we consult a concordance about Apollos, the first reference we find is this one in the book of Acts:

> Now a Jew named Apollos, an Alexandrian by birth, an eloquent man, came to Ephesus; and he was mighty in the Scriptures. This man had been instructed in the way of the Lord; and being fervent in spirit, he was speaking and teaching accurately the things concerning Jesus, being acquainted only with the baptism of John; and he began to speak out boldly in the synagogue. But when Priscilla and Aquila heard him, they took him aside and explained to him the way of God more accurately. And when he wanted to go across to Achaia, the brethren encouraged him and wrote to the disciples to welcome him; and when he had arrived, he greatly helped those who had believed through grace, for he powerfully refuted the Jews in public, demonstrating by the Scriptures that Jesus was the Christ.
>
> It happened that while Apollos was at Corinth, Paul passed through the upper country and came to Ephesus. (Acts 18:24–19:1)

We learn from this passage several potentially helpful things: (1) Apollos went to Corinth after Paul had started the church there, Paul was not in Corinth at the time, and Apollos had not yet spoken with Paul. (2) When Apollos arrived at Corinth, he greatly helped "those who had believed through grace." (3) Apollos was eloquent, mighty in the Scriptures, and a powerful debater. Thus we have a little clearer picture of what the situation was in Corinth. After Paul left Corinth, Apollos showed up and made a powerful impression on the Corinthians—certainly with his skill at debating the Jews and presumably with his eloquence as well.

How did Apollos compare in the minds of the Corinthians with the great apostle whom he had replaced? We get some evidence of that if we comb through both of Paul's letters to Corinth. In 2 Corinthians 10–13 we find Paul using the sternest words he ever used with anybody in Scripture. This whole section is a painful defense of his apostolic ministry, which Paul undertook because many at Corinth had judged him and found him inadequate. For our purposes, these two statements are the most interesting:

> They say [of Paul], "His letters are weighty and strong, but his personal presence is unimpressive and his speech contemptible." (2 Corinthians 10:10)

> I consider myself not in the least inferior to the most eminent apostles. But even if I am unskilled in speech, yet I am not so in knowledge; in fact, in every way we have made this evident to you in all things. (2 Corinthians 11:5-6)

Many of the Corinthians found Paul to be inferior to the other apostles, especially in his unimpressive way of talking and teaching. Paul reminded them that even if he was a poor speaker (which he was not admitting), there was nothing wrong with his knowledge—the knowledge of the gospel given to him by revelation from Christ Himself.

So we know that Apollos was an eloquent and persuasive speaker who was well received by the Corinthians, and we know that Paul was judged to be an unskilled and unimpressive speaker whom they were inclined to dismiss. Now we want to take this information and see if it helps us to find a coherent message in the early chapters of 1 Corinthians. Does this information help us? I think it does. Notice in the following excerpts how certain questions keep coming up: (1) Why did Paul speak with such unimpressive simplicity when he came to them? (2) Did Paul's speech really qualify as wisdom? (3) How were the Corinthians to judge Paul?

Christ did not send me to baptize, but to preach the
gospel, *not in cleverness of speech.* (1 Corinthians
1:17, emphasis added)

When I came to you, brethren, I did not come with
superiority of speech or of wisdom. (1 Corinthians 2:1,
emphasis added)

I was with you in weakness and in fear and in much
trembling, and my message and my preaching were
not in persuasive words of wisdom. (1 Corinthians
2:3-4, emphasis added)

Yet we do speak *wisdom* among those who are
mature. (1 Corinthians 2:6, emphasis added)

I, brethren, [when I was last among you,] *could not
speak to you as to spiritual men,* but as to men of
flesh, as to infants in Christ. (1 Corinthians 3:1,
emphasis added)

Let a man *regard us in this manner,* as servants of
Christ and stewards of the mysteries of God. . . . But
to me it is a very small thing *that I may be examined by you.* . . . Therefore *do not go on passing
judgment* before the time. (1 Corinthians 4:1,3,5,
emphasis added)

Our search for the coherent argument of this passage
should cause us to notice two repeating themes in the first
four chapters: (1) People were splitting up into factions, choosing sides between Apollos and Paul, especially. (2) Paul kept
referring to his own simple speech and defending it as true
wisdom. Having seen these things, then, the background information that Apollos was considered eloquent and Paul was

considered uncouth helps fill in the picture wonderfully. Paul kept defending his unspectacular way of speaking because it was exactly that which some Corinthians were holding against him. They preferred the powerfully persuasive style of Apollos, which to them sounded the way wisdom ought to sound. We could fill in this picture further by going outside the Bible to get some understanding of what the Greek notion of wisdom would likely have been. But these simple pieces of information about Paul and Apollos, gained from the Bible itself, are enough to help us recreate the framework within which four whole chapters were written.

GETTING THE TRUE STORY

AUTHORS AND READERS usually gain their common knowledge through common experience. It does not take research and scholarship; they just pick it up naturally as they live their .lives, because they live in similar environments. But you and I do not live in the same world that Moses and Jeremiah and Jesus and Paul lived in. There is a one-way door out of those times and places, and we are irrevocably on the outside. Compared with the original readers, we are at a disadvantage. Not a total disadvantage, though. We know some things already, and some others we can learn.

For our purposes, there are three different kinds of knowledge, with three different strategies for getting that knowledge:

- Human knowledge. *Definition:* the knowledge that every human being has just by virtue of being human. *Examples:* hunger, fatigue, love, peer pressure, blood, cool water, hot bread, and headaches. *How to get human knowledge:* from a human being—yourself or anyone else.
- Cultural knowledge. *Definition:* the knowledge that comes from living in a particular culture at a particular

time and place. *Examples:* Velcro, PTA meetings, soft-
ware, public television, Sunday school, and aluminum
recycling. *How to get cultural knowledge:* from anyone
who lives in the culture.
- Personal knowledge. *Definition:* the knowledge that
comes from personal interaction. *Examples:* my middle
name, the way to my house, which tool I borrowed
from David Crabtree yesterday, the story about my
brief Little League career, my theology, and how I treat
my children. *How to get personal knowledge:* only from
those who know the person.

All three of these kinds of knowledge can be important in
communication. The biblical authors at times expected all three
from their readers. When the Gospel writers told the story of
Jesus walking on the water, no one bothered to explain that
people usually sink. That's an example of human knowledge.
Jesus' Jewish audience viewed Samaritans as racially and reli-
giously tainted, and Jesus capitalized on that when He chose
the hero of the story of the Good Samaritan. That's an example,
on Jesus' part, of reliance on cultural knowledge. While
explaining to the Thessalonians about "the man of lawlessness," Paul wrote, "Do you not remember that while I was still
with you, I was telling you these things? And you know what
restrains him now, so that in his time he will be revealed"
(2 Thessalonians 2:5-6). Paul had an expectation among his
readers of personal knowledge.

THE CHALLENGE OF
HISTORICAL RESEARCH

WE MODERN READERS of the Bible have two strikes against
us: although we are human beings and we share the knowledge that all humans have, we do not live in the biblical culture and we do not know the people of the Bible personally.

We do not start out knowing the things the biblical authors expected their audience to know. If we want to make up this deficit, we must turn to those who did live in that culture and did know the biblical figures personally. We cannot talk to them, but they can talk to us. In the writings and artifacts that have survived the centuries, the ancients have told parts of their story. We need to read their mail. We need to eavesdrop. The historical scholar is a professional eavesdropper. Such eavesdropping in old texts is the best solution to the knowledge gap between us and the intended readers of Scripture.

It must be admitted, however, that eavesdropping is not as easy or reliable a way to gain information as we would like. My own cultural and personal knowledge has been gained through constant, minute-by-minute, day-by-day experience. I have ingested huge amounts of data, and I have done it without even trying. Eavesdropping in an ancient text is hard work. I have to dig. I also have to worry much more about whether the "fact" that I have dug up is true. I have to think hard.

There are unavoidable limitations on us when we do historical research. To work wisely with the background requires us to understand these limits. What is it going to take to ensure that I have eavesdropped well, that the facts I come away with are true? Most of us do not live our lives doing historical research. But every student of the Bible can profit from understanding the strengths and limitations of background research.

Limited Sources

My potential sources of information are limited to those who actually knew the fact I am looking for. The author knew it, of course, and I can always comb through the text looking for clues. Otherwise, it depends on how many other people knew. At any given moment, the author might have been relying on knowledge shared by his entire culture, by a subculture, by a large group who knew him, by a small group who knew him, or by one other person. As the size of the pool dwindles, so does the number of texts I can reasonably expect to give me information. I can find many sources that talk about Jewish-Samaritan relations, including several authors in the Bible, because so many people knew about them. But where would I go to find out what Paul taught the Thessalonians about the "man of lawlessness"? The group of people to whom he talked about this mysterious figure was relatively small, and as far as I know, none of them wrote about the subject. Historical research will not help. If I cannot deduce it from the text itself, then I must be content not to know.

Limited Reporting

Even if I have texts written by people who knew the facts, I cannot count on them to tell me. Other people's eyes and ears are serving for mine; I cannot turn them in the direction I want to look. I am forced to read what they were interested in talking about, not what I am interested in learning. Often we need specific kinds of information but can find no one who wrote about it, at least not in the detail we need. Paul mentioned the practice of baptism for the dead, but I have never found anyone close to Paul's time and circle who described what that was. Presumably, every New Testament author was familiar with this practice, but no one wrote it down. I am stuck.

Disjointed and Simplistic Data

Reality is complicated. The best historical scholars know enough to realize how much they do not know. Ancient texts give us little bits and pieces of a much larger picture. We amateur historians face the danger of forgetting this. We are prone to generalize too quickly on evidence too slim to bear the weight of our conclusions. We turn a letter from a soldier griping about army life into "a deep-seated antimilitaristic sentiment among the populace." We then turn around and use this generalization to analyze everything else. This makes for poor history and even worse interpretation. When I interpret a text,

I am dealing with one specific person (the author), not an abstract generality. The realities of that person's world were fully as intricate as the realities of my own. Could some future historian see into the complexities of my mind by reading a few newspapers and a handful of my letters? I cannot see how. The spottiness of our historical data forces us to be ruthlessly realistic about what we can know 'and what we cannot. For a student of the Bible, settling for no story at all is much better than weaving a fairy tale.

The Necessity of Interpretation

Because our information is coming from texts, it is only as good as our interpretation of the texts. This is true both of language studies and of background studies. The ancients cannot tell us about their language or their culture if we misinterpret what they are saying. Any scholar who tells you that X was true of an ancient culture is really giving you his interpretation of ancient texts. There is an exegetical conclusion lurking behind every historical fact we have. That is not bad; I am not accusing anyone of being sneaky or underhanded. It is just a fact. We have no choice—to establish the truth of a historical claim, we must establish the validity of the interpretation that led to it.

The Necessity of Deduction

Much of what we know of the ancient world we have not been told—we deduced it. For every interesting fact some ancient author gave us, there are countless more he knew but did not bother to write down. After all, the people he was writing to knew them already. But our hunger for knowledge goes beyond what we have been told. The only ones who can tell us are the ones who were there, but what if they do not speak up? What can we do with eyewitnesses who will not testify? We do what any good detective would do with an uncooperative witness—we take what he did say and deduce what he did not say. This is perfectly acceptable and necessary, but it does provide one more hurdle to overcome in our search for the facts of history. Our "facts" are only as good as the deductions that led to them.

Such detective work does have its dangers, but I do not want to overemphasize them. We can get good results. Anyone who has ever stepped into the middle of a conversation knows how this works. Suppose I wander over to a group of friends who are deep into a discussion. They all know what the topic of discussion is, but I do not. Frank says, "I used to fly all the time, but I hardly ever do anymore." *Hmm. Does he mean as a pilot or a passenger? And anyway, I do not remember Frank doing much flying. What is he talking about?* Thelma replies, "I still do, but I have to flap my arms a lot more than I used to." *Now this is getting bizarre. Maybe they are talking about hang gliding? No, you do not flap your arms in hang gliding. Paper airplanes? Maybe they are using metaphors. I do not get it yet.* Arlene says, "I always find myself sitting down to take the final in a class that I haven't attended all year." *Aha! Now I know what they are talking about. They are talking about dreams. Flying dreams, either flapping or nonflapping, and school dreams are some of the most common ones. Now it all makes sense.* Gathering my courage and trusting my deduction, I jump into the conversation to recount the dream I had last night. If my thinking was right, I am rewarded with sympathetic nods; if not, I get blank stares.

In effect, when we read books of the Bible, we are jumping into an ongoing conversation. We play detective. We find ourselves saying, "If X was true, then this all comes together." The dangers are real. We can be hasty in our deductions and conclude things that were not true. But if we proceed carefully, much can be accomplished. We are not just "guessing." To a certain extent, we cannot help but do this. Reconstructing the background in this way is part of the larger process of making coherent sense of the passage, and we *must* do this.

If we do not develop this skill, we will never be good readers of the Bible or any other book.

Reliance on Other Scholars

Most of us have neither the time nor the expertise to do all our own research, and we must rely on the eavesdropping, interpretations, and deductions of those who do. This is not bad. Much good work has been done, and it would be foolish not to take advantage of it. But it would not take much looking to discover that for any particular historical question there are usually several different scholarly points of view. This should not surprise us, given what we have just been talking about. Scholarship is eavesdropping limited by the quality of the exegesis and deduction that accompany it. Historical "facts" are really conclusions based on interpretation and reasoning. We cannot afford to be naïve about this. As much as we might wish it were otherwise, we cannot assume that everything we read in a reference book is true.

This puts us into something of a bind. We went to the scholars in the first place because we did not have the time or expertise to get the information for ourselves. Do we now need the time and expertise to check every statement in every book we read? No, clearly not. As far as time is concerned, it would be highly impractical to expect that anyone could check every statement in every reference book. No one has time, not even other scholars. But we do have time to be cautious about historical claims that have a big impact on the meaning of the biblical text. If some scholar claimed to have incontrovertible evidence that Jesus' bones were lying in a grave outside Jerusalem, you can bet that many of us would find the time to check it out. We take the time we have and concentrate on the most important questions first.

As for expertise, we do not want to exaggerate the differences between the scholar and the layperson. Any reasonably intelligent person can enter into a mental dialogue with a reference book. After all, scholars are those who (1) know how to find historical evidence, (2) use exegesis to interpret the relevant texts, and (3) draw conclusions from the texts they have interpreted. Their biggest advantage over the layperson is in knowing how to find historical evidence. If they tell us what evidence they found, then we can join them in the process of exegesis and reasoning from that evidence. How successful we are at this will vary according to our skill and experience. Here are a few pieces of advice:

1. Separate evidence from conclusions. Even when scholars have not reasoned well from the evidence, they have done us a service if they have shown us that evidence. But we must be careful to discern whether we are really looking at evidence. A line quoted from an ancient text is evidence. The statement "This is the way they did things back then" is not. It is a conclusion. It may be right; it may be wrong. It may have direct evidence to back it up, or it may be a deduction the scholar has drawn. Suppose I read the following two lines in some hypothetical work of scholarship:

- "The Essenes did not trust women to be faithful."
- "John the Baptist did not trust women to be faithful."

These two statements sound very much the same, but in my hypothetical example they actually spring from different sources. The first statement is just a restatement of what Josephus, a first-century writer, said about the Essenes, and he was in a pretty good position to know. Our scholar did not give the evidence, but strong evidence lies behind his statement. The second statement, however, is a work of reasoning by our hypothetical scholar. His thinking runs like this: (1) John the Baptist was an Essene; (2) John the Baptist denounced Herodias for marrying her first husband's brother; therefore, (3) John the Baptist, like the Essenes, did not trust women to be faithful. Our scholar did not explain all this; he just gave his conclusion. Maybe he had explained it in a journal article somewhere, and he did not want to repeat himself. But because he did not spell it out, I do not know why he says what he does. If I knew his thinking, I might want to argue back. Maybe I am not convinced that John the Baptist was an Essene. Maybe I would not find John's denunciation of Herodias sufficient evidence that he mistrusted all women. But because I have not heard the scholar's argument, I do not know what to think. What I can do is make a mental note that I have not yet heard an explanation for why I should accept this claim.

2. Critique exegesis and reasoning. There is no necessary connection between historical knowledge and exegetical skill. Some scholars have an astounding grasp of historical facts, know their way through a library better than they know their way home, and yet are not particularly skilled interpreters. Some have not received the training in it; others do not have the interest or the skill. Do not be cowed by their superior knowledge. Critique their thinking. If, in spite of the evidence they present, their arguments are not convincing, then remain unconvinced. On the other hand, we do not want to be maliciously skeptical. There are many scholars who think extremely well about the evidence they amass. What we must do is humbly insist that everyone's arguments, whether scholarly or not, make sense.

3. Be aware of presuppositions. As we have seen, reasoning from evidence plays a large part in historical studies. Such reasoning is built upon the foundation of the scholar's presuppositions. If I know that I do not share the scholar's operating assumptions, I know enough to examine his conclusions with special care. Unfortunately, scholars do not always spell out their presuppositions or the role those presuppositions play in any conclusions. It is important that we try to find out.

People have a tendency to see historical scholarship as an objective, "scientific" discipline. If we mean by this that there is a certain amount of objective evidence to consider, then I agree. But if we fall into the trap of thinking that subjective human judgments play no part in it, we severely mislead ourselves. This is not—and cannot—be true. Presuppositions control conclusions here as much as anywhere else. Scholarship is based on the exercise of informed judgment. If a scholar has poor judgment, then he will take good data and draw poor conclusions. If we are going to think clearly about the "facts" presented to us, we must be prepared to consider the biases of the scholar whose work we are reading.

I have no desire in my preceding comments to foster an attitude of cynicism or skepticism about works of scholarship. We all owe so much to the laborious work that many have exerted over the years that we could not begin to repay our debt. But a certain insistent attitude of "I will believe it when you have explained to me why I should" is entirely appropriate. We care about the truth. That is why we must hold our teachers answerable to that truth.

THE RELEVANCE OF BACKGROUND INFORMATION

A LOT OF hard work goes into digging out the facts of history. When anyone, scholar or layperson, expends all that effort, there is a natural temptation to fall in love with the fact discovered. "I've got a fact, and I've got to use it!" But getting hold of a true historical fact is only half the battle for the exegete. An exegete gathers data only to throw most of it away again. What drives us is the desire for facts that significantly affect the meaning of the text. It is not enough to determine that a piece of data is true; it is equally important to determine whether it is relevant.

To move from "Yes, this is a true fact" to "Yes, this fact affects my interpretation," two important questions must be answered:

Question 1: Did This Fact Belong to the Author's Culture?
In order for a historical fact to qualify as relevant background information, it must be more than "old news"; it must be part of the specific world that the author and the original readers lived in. That is what we mean by background in the first place: it is something that the author knew or believed but did not explain because he expected the readers to know it or believe it, too. That is why it is so important that we not read our twenty-first-century cultural ideas into the Bible; they clearly could not have been part of the original readers' thinking. But not every aspect of ancient cultures was part of the original readers' thinking either. The specific time, place, religious tradition, and so forth in which a particular person lives determines the mental map he steers by.

In my community there has been a battle between environmentalists and loggers over the logging of old-growth timber, the preferred habitat of the spotted owl. Two environmentalists talking to each other about the "spotted owl problem" expect to conjure up certain images in each other's minds. Their thoughts are of an endangered species whose habitat is being threatened by greed and shortsightedness, and they feel protectiveness and pity. Two loggers talking on the same subject have different expectations of each other. For them the problem is the loss of jobs, and the appropriate feelings are those of rage and resentment. An environmentalist and a logger cannot talk to each other with the same expectations. And future archaeologists finding a letter from my community would not immediately know how to interpret a statement like "I just shot a spotted owl." They might conclude the writer must be prostrate with grief over killing this valuable bird. Well, that depends on whether they are reading a letter from an environmentalist or the logger who lives next door.

To illustrate this point, let us look at just one piece of evidence concerning the issue of women's head coverings. In order to understand Paul's point in 1 Corinthian 11, it would be helpful to know what the women's practice was and its significance. In the Babylonian Talmud we find the following statement: "Men sometimes cover their heads and sometimes not; but women's hair is always covered, and children are always bareheaded."[2] This is clearly a helpful piece of the puzzle. But what exactly is its significance for our passage? There are any number of hoops this little fact has to jump through before it can be called relevant to the 1 Corinthians 11 passage. First of all, we have to recognize that the rabbinic literature—the Mishnah, the Talmud, and so forth—was compiled much later than the time of the New Testament. Some of its observations reach back to the time of the New Testament and before, but much of it reflects post-temple Jewish culture several centuries later. There is no doubt that at some point a long time ago the Jewish practice was for women to cover their hair, but it is not a foregone conclusion that they did so in New Testament times.

Even if we were confident that this was indeed Jewish practice at the time when Paul wrote, its relevance is still debatable. After all, Paul was writing to people in Corinth, a large Greek city. Paul seems to have been concerned with the cultural message that a woman was sending by uncovering her head, but which cultural standard was the relevant one? Corinth was a Gentile town, unconcerned with Jewish standards. Then again, the church first met in the house of Titius Justus, a God-fearing Gentile. The God-fearers were Gentiles who believed in Yahweh and frequented the synagogues to hear more about Him. We can speculate that the God-fearers may have adopted some Jewish cultural perspectives. One of the important families in the church was that of Crispus, the Jewish leader of the synagogue. Finally, the one who was advocating this practice was Paul, a Jew (but a Jew who was raised outside Palestine).

Not for a minute are we questioning the truth of the Talmud's observation that Jewish women covered their hair. What we are wrestling with is whether that was a part of the

Corinthians' world. Such questions are not always easy to answer, but they must be asked. Sometimes we will be able to demonstrate to ourselves and others that a certain thing was indeed known to the author and his readers. Other times we will not. In such cases it is better to know that we do not know than to assume blindly that the background issues have been settled.

Question 2: Does the Context Require This Fact's Use?

Let us suppose that some particular fact has passed every test we have described so far. Its truth is beyond question. And the people who were aware of this fact clearly included the author and readers of our text. Have we reached the end of our quest? Has the relevance of this fact for the interpretation of our passage been clearly established? Not yet. The final and most important test remains: the test of the context.

Context has exactly the same effect on background knowledge that it has on language conventions. We have seen previously how words can have more than one meaning, and we have seen that context shows which meaning the author intended. If someone tells me that I left the faucet running, I do not immediately picture the spigot jogging around the bathroom. I start out knowing several meanings for the word *running,* but once I hear the context, I think only of the one that fits. The same thing is true of background knowledge. I have vast quantities of facts and beliefs stored up in my head, but I do not trot them all out every time I interpret what someone says to me. When my son was younger, he used to sleep on the top of a bunk bed. I knew this fact about him, but I did not use this piece of knowledge every time he said anything. If he told me he was going to ride his bike, his bunk bed would not even come to mind; if he told me he had just fallen out of bed, it would.

What we have to fight, with all of our mental energy, is the idea that a particular piece of background information imposes a meaning on the text. This is not true. Context and background work together, with context casting the deciding vote. Even when a particular piece of background information is strikingly obvious and well known, it still may not be relevant. Consider the lowly chair. Everybody knows what a chair is for—it is for sitting in. Years of field study have brought me to the same conclusion time and time again: people sit in chairs. Undeniably, it is true and everybody knows it: chairs are to sit in. Still, is that *always* the most relevant piece of information about a chair? Does "sitting" come to mind every time a chair gets mentioned? Consider the following scenarios:

- *First scenario:* My wife and I are trying to reach a copy of *Wuthering Heights* on the top shelf of our bookcase. *My wife says:* "Here's a chair." Background information: A chair is a solid piece of furniture that will support my weight. *She means:* Stand on this and hand me the book.
- *Second scenario:* My wife and I are being chased by a bad guy who wants to separate us from our cash and our lives. I am casting my eyes around frantically for something with which to defend myself. *My wife says:* "Here's a chair." Background information: A chair is light enough for me to pick up and yet fairly massive. *She means:* Pick up the chair and bean this guy.
- *Third scenario:* My wife and I are in the first landing party on the surface of Mars. We are walking around on the desolate surface, looking for evidence of extraterrestrial life. *My wife says:* "Here's a chair." Background information: A chair is not a natural formation. It is an artifact made by living beings. *She means:* Set your phaser on stun; I think we've got company.

Although chairs are intended for sitting, in each scenario my wife would be flabbergasted if I sat down. Yes, I am aware that chairs are made for sitting, but I know other things about them as well. What I think of when someone says "chair" to me depends on the context.

So far, my examples are simple and obvious and perhaps (yes, I admit it) silly. But there is an extremely important point at the back of them, one that is tricky and subtle in practice. To illustrate this point, I want to look briefly at a real-life interpretive issue. In James 5:11 we read, "We count those blessed who endured. You have heard of the endurance of Job and have seen the outcome of the Lord's dealings, that the Lord is full of compassion and is merciful." One line of reasoning on this passage points out that *The Testament of Job,* an extrabiblical text, portrays Job as exercising great charity to the poor. According to this argument, James expected his audience to remember this part of the Job tradition and to read it into his words. In this verse about Job, therefore, two themes from James' letter come together: charity toward the poor and perseverance. I want to make clear that I have no problem with a claim that James might have expected his readers to supply some background themselves; this can and does happen. And I am willing to admit that this extrabiblical tradition could have been known by James and his readers. I disagree, however, with the conclusion that this tradition could have any relevance to James 5:11. It does not matter that such a tradition existed. It does not matter that James discussed charity to the poor in his letter. What matters is how his specific words show me what he intended. James was in the middle of an admonition to persevere in faith. He pointed to the perseverance of the prophets. He reminded his readers of the blessings of those who had persevered in the past. He then reminded them of "the endurance of Job." He was not inviting them to consider everything they knew about Job. He was inviting them to consider Job's endurance. From the perspective of how language works, an invitation to consider Job's endurance was an invitation *not* to consider his charity. Fundamentally, communication is not an additive process; it is a subtractive one. An author's context pares away all the possible meanings and connotations of things until only that which the author wanted is left.

For some reason, metaphorical language often seems to inspire us to violate this rule. When we are told that something is "like X," something in us longs to stuff X full of everything we know about it. We need to fight this urge. Jesus said, "You are the salt of the earth" (Matthew 5:13). He did not mean to suggest that everything that is true about salt is true of us. It does not matter that the readers knew a hundred different things about salt. What I want to know is, of all the things they knew about salt, which of them did Jesus have in mind? The context is the only way I can answer that. I have got to get control of runaway "backgrounditis" before I start saying things like "Fact 63 about salt: saltwater leaves a white deposit behind when it evaporates. And we, too, when we die and 'evaporate' from this world, should leave behind a deposit of good works." I made this up, of course, and I mean it to sound far-fetched. I hope it does.

BACKGROUND INFORMATION AND JAMES 5:13-20

THE WARNINGS WE have been discussing are relevant to the passage under discussion throughout this book: James 5:13-20. In the previous chapter I asserted that sickness is not the issue in James 5; weakness and weariness in the struggle of faith are at the heart of the matter. Context strongly supports that reading of the text as the most likely. But does the available background information support that conclusion? It might seem that it does not. Most commentaries on James amass evidence for two aspects of the culture that seem to support the traditional view: (1) There were cultural connections among anointing, exorcism of demons, and supernatural healing of sickness. (2) There was a cultural belief that sickness was a result of sin. Commentaries do not exactly use these facts to argue for their interpretation. Few commentaries even acknowledge that there is any other way to take the passage. But they all assert the *relevance* of these facts to James 5.

My argument all along has been that the *context* tells the reader when background facts are relevant; the background does not impose a meaning on the text. This is true as well in James 5. Suppose that it could be demonstrated historically (which it cannot) that James' readers regularly practiced the anointing of the sick and *only* of the sick. Would that mean that James had to have been talking about sickness? I do not think so, not if the context were strong enough. If the context clearly shows that James was talking about moral weariness, then James would be saying, in effect, "You who have been invoking the power of God for sick people by anointing them, you should also be praying for and anointing those who have a much more significant debility: weariness in the struggle of faith."

But the available evidence is not enough to prove that anointing was used only for the sick. We know that anointing was used in many kinds of situations. Jesus reminded a Pharisee that he could have honored Jesus (but did not) by anointing Jesus' head when He came into the Pharisee's house. Anointing had a long-standing symbolic significance, marking kings, priests, altars, and so forth as having a special relationship with God. Clearly the same understanding of anointing that led to anointing the sick could easily have led to anointing anyone who was suffering and needed the special work of God in his life. We do not have enough evidence to say with any certainty how the churches looked at anointing at the time James wrote.

The cultural evidence concerning sickness and sin is even more problematic. I have been frustrated in dealing with commentaries on James in the past. Although most of them refer to the cultural belief that sickness is a result of sin, they often do not say why they see that as relevant. Are they suggesting that James himself believed that sickness was a result of sin? There is evidence that some people near and after the time of the New Testament believed that sickness resulted from sin. But even if that were a common part of James' culture, are we saying that James followed his culture in this belief and taught it as truth in the Bible? We have many other examples of the apostles fighting against the superstitious and gullible thinking of their culture; why would we think any differently of James? In fact, James explicitly said, *"If* he has committed sins . . . ," implying that sin may or may not have been involved. There were elements in the culture that connected sickness with sin, but there is nothing in the context of James 5 that makes this relevant to his argument, even if we agreed that sickness was James' topic.

Before we leave the issue of the background for James 5, it will be helpful to think a bit about the theological background. Can it really be that the apostles believed that God has promised to heal us from sickness? That He does so at times is undeniable. That He will one day heal all of us totally is part of our great hope. But James would be saying more than that; he would be claiming that the prayers of the elders are effective now, that God hears such prayers and will heal now in answer to them. Does other biblical evidence support this? Does our experience support this? Other biblical references to healing can best be understood as referring to our great hope of total healing one day; this passage alone would be claiming that healing has been promised to us now. I do not see the Bible making this claim elsewhere. I do not see Christian communities filled with people whose every illness has been eliminated by elder anointing. I do not believe this is a reasonable theological background to bring to James 5.

On the other hand, the promise that God will aid Christians struggling with their faith is very much a part of apostolic thinking. For one thing, James himself claimed that God uses trials to teach us perseverance. So did Paul in Romans 5. James said that God gives wisdom to those who ask Him. The author of Hebrews reminded us of God's discipline and how it yields the peaceful fruit of righteousness. And we are to look after each other in this regard. John, in 1 John, boldly proclaimed that we can confidently pray that God would give life to a brother caught in sin. The promise of God's encouragement and help in the midst of present struggles is a strong theme in the Bible. If indeed that is what James was talking about, his theme resonates with the rest of his letter and the rest of Scripture.

CONCLUSION

LANGUAGE STUDIES AND background studies are both the handmaidens of contextual interpretation. They do not dictate; they serve. They help provide the raw materials out of which the author expected to build his vision in the minds of his readers. They do not impose a meaning on the text; the author pulled his meaning out of them. However, if we substitute bogus for real materials, if we know the wrong language and the wrong background, we can miss what the author was trying to say. These realities of interpretation give us three foundational principles for background studies:

1. We must constantly be wary that we are not reading our own misplaced background assumptions into the text.
2. We should try to learn as much as we can about the biblical world, but cautiously, taking care that our facts are really facts.
3. We must subject any background facts we bring to the text to the ruthless scrutiny of the context.

It all comes back to the author and the context he created. With language and background studies we truly are eavesdropping. We are trying to sneak out of various texts information that the authors never intended to give us. But when we concentrate on the actual context of the passage we are studying, then we have the author working with us. He wanted as much to be understood as we want to understand. As we struggle to pull his meaning out of the text, he is on the other side pushing. His mental effort went into putting his words together such that others could see for themselves what he was thinking. Our mental effort must go into reconstructing those thoughts. Although we are not the readers he envisioned, our best hope of understanding the author does not lie in language and background studies. Our best hope lies in our God-given capacity to think.

STUDY QUESTIONS

1. In John 1:29, John the Baptist said, "Behold, the Lamb of God who takes away the sin of the world!" The word *lamb* is simple enough to understand, but what is the background information shared by John and his hearers that informed this unusual statement? (This and the following questions require the use of Bible reference books, such as Bible encyclopedias, histories, and commentaries. These, of course, must be used critically.)

2. Read Paul's letters to the Ephesians, the Colossians, and Philemon. What is the connection among these letters? Under what circumstances did Paul write them? To whom were they written, and how did the letters get there?

3. One of the passages obviously affected by cultural background information is Paul's discussion in 1 Corinthians 11 of women wearing head coverings and shaving their heads.

   a. Find whatever information you can about the practice and significance of head coverings and head shaving in Paul's day. Notice which information seems to be deduced from 1 Corinthians and which seems to be derived from outside historical evidence.

b. Does the information you gathered help you understand 1 Corinthians 11? How?

4. An important background issue in the study of Paul's letter to the Galatians centers upon when and under what circumstances Paul wrote the letter. There are two competing theories, known as the "Northern Galatian Hypothesis" and the "Southern Galatian Hypothesis." Explore this issue by taking the following steps:

a. Read the article on Galatians from *The Zondervan Pictorial Encyclopedia of the Bible* (or some other good Bible encyclopedia) to familiarize yourself with the issue.

b. If you have time and access to a good library, consult several commentaries on Galatians to see what the arguments on both sides are.

c. Compare Paul's chronology in the first two chapters of Galatians with the events in the book of Acts. Construct a side-by-side list matching events in Galatians with those in Acts in a way that fits the Northern Galatian Hypothesis. Construct a new side-by-side list that fits the Southern Galatian Hypothesis.

d. Decide for yourself whether the context of Galatians gives us enough evidence to decide between the two options.

CHAPTER SIX

Building a Biblical Worldview

It was all very well to say "Drink me," but the wise little Alice
was not going to do *that* in a hurry. "No, I'll look first," she said,
"and see whether it's marked 'poison' or not"; for she had read
several nice stories about children who had got burnt, and
eaten up by wild beasts and other unpleasant things, all
because they *would* not remember the simple rules their friends
had taught them: such as, that a red-hot poker will burn you if
you hold it too long; and that if you cut your finger *very* deeply
with a knife, it usually bleeds; and she had never forgotten that,
if you drink from a bottle marked "poison," it is almost certain
to disagree with you, sooner or later.

EVERY DAY I THINK of questions I would dearly like God
to answer. And these are not questions generated by an idle
curiosity; they are serious, vital questions. As I sit here writing,
I have questions plaguing me. Let me briefly list a few of them:

- I have the ability to apply great pressure on myself to
  get things done. But I do not have the ability to control that pressure. Sometimes I put so much pressure
  on myself that I get physically ill. How can I learn to
  relax, to release that self-inflicted pressure?
- Our children's soccer club has been using our pasture
  for soccer practices and games. Our neighbor complained to the county about this use of the field, and

the county demanded that we close the field. How ought I relate to my neighbor in light of his actions against us?

• I am convinced that male headship is a biblical concept. But how is it to be exercised? What is the nature of that authority, and how do I use it responsibly, lovingly? ("You bought what?!")

I have often wished I could sit down and talk to God over a cup of coffee. I would explain to Him the various difficulties I am currently facing in my life, and He would give me thoughtful advice. Life is hard. It presents us with many problems. Issues arise that are urgent, vitally important, and unique. We all yearn for God's counsel.

This puts us in a terrible predicament. We badly want God to address our unique, personal problems. But when we turn to our best source for answers to our questions, the Bible, we find God's advice to others. What is worse, the recipients of this advice were members of different cultures who lived thousands of years ago. Much of what God told them is wasted on me. How can the Bible be made to address my unique problems?

There is a gap between what we find in Scripture—God addressing the problems of people in another culture—and what I, personally, want to hear from Him. It's a gap between interpretation and application. If this gap can be bridged, all of the work involved in Bible study becomes well worth the effort.

The next two chapters outline how we can bridge this gap. The discussion is based on one assumption: there is a well-established method for moving from interpretation to application, one that every human being knows and uses. The argument of this chapter will appeal to your common sense. The method described is one everyone uses every day. It is so familiar that we go through the process without being conscious of what we are doing. But we need to make this method explicit so that we can use it with the Bible.

THE PROCESS IN OVERVIEW

MOVING FROM INTERPRETATION to application means taking the commands and the teachings God gave to other people and using this information to predict what God wants *us* to do. Where do we use this sort of process in our everyday lives? This happens in any number of situations: an employee takes commands and instruction from his employer and uses these to predict what his employer wants him to do in other situations; a student second-guesses his teacher; a husband would like to be able to predict his wife's reactions to things. And there are other examples. But probably the best example (and the one I will use) is a child's prediction of his parent's wishes.

The task that faces a child who wants to act in obedience to a parent is similar to that which faces a believer with respect to God. A child listens to commands and instruction from his parents. He observes what they do in various circumstances. He gains experience of life. And on the basis of this information he must learn to predict what obedience to his parent entails in various situations. This is like what a believer must do to be obedient to God. On the basis of what he reads in Scripture, a believer must determine what God wants him to do. In both cases an individual must use limited information to predict the response of another to an unlimited number of situations.

Let us look at what a child does. From day one, a child begins to develop an understanding of how the universe operates. A child must sort through the collage of color that is before him and learn to distinguish his mother's face from the wallpaper, his bottle from his thumb. After a period of observation, he is ready to posit his first guess. He then needs to test and retest this guess until he is certain that that particular

164 | The Language of God

combination of colors and spots is his mother's face. It is not easy. Sometimes the eyes and lips are different colors. Sometimes the hair is free-flowing; other times it is covered. But the child can, with time, sort it all out. When he can pick out his mother's face consistently, he moves on to the next problem. Slowly but surely, he constructs an understanding of the world and how the world works. This is his preunderstanding.

An important part of the child's understanding of the world is how his parents view the world. If he acts in ways that do not conform with his parents' principles, he will be punished. So he needs to construct a model of his parents' worldview in his own mind. He needs to know their whole system of beliefs: what they like, what they do not like, what they consider important, what is not important, what they believe to be true, what is not true, and so forth. The better his model of his parents' understanding, the better he will be able to anticipate their response, and the better he will be able to spare his posterior undue discomfort.

Once a child has constructed a reliable model of his parent's worldview, he can view any situation that comes along through the parent's eyes. He can predict what actions his parent would approve and disapprove. Therefore, to live in accordance with his parent's worldview would be to apply the parent's worldview.

Just as a parent has a worldview that he would like his child to adopt and apply constantly, so God has a worldview that He would like man to adopt. God would like nothing better than for man to abandon his self-centeredness and embrace God's own perspective on the universe. God's perspective on the universe is what we call "truth." Every statement that describes part of God's perspective is one component of truth. If we could compile a list of statements that comprehensively describes all of God's perspective, that list would be a description of truth. If we knew truth, we could determine what God wants us to do in any circumstance of life.

Therefore, as Christians, our job is the same as a child's. Using the information available to us, we need to construct a model of God's worldview so that we can look at the world through His eyes. We need to know as much as possible about how God understands reality: how it works, how it is put together, why it is the way it is, and so forth. If we have a good, complete model of God's worldview, then we can apply that worldview to any situation. I am going to refer to our model of God's worldview as our "theology." I will use this word in a broader sense than the word usually includes; I will use it to refer to the study of God's view of all reality and its implications. In other words, *theology*, as I will use it, is the study of truth—all truth. When we construct a theology, we are assembling a model of the way things really are.

So then, just as a child constructs a model of what his parent believes to be true, what he considers important, and so forth, so Christians need to build a theology (in the sense that I have just defined) that reflects God's perspective on reality. Once we have a good, sound theology, we can predict how God would advise us. Now we need to look at how a child constructs his model, and we will learn some things that will help us build a trustworthy theology.

THE STEPS OF THE PROCESS

HOW DOES A child build his model? He builds it the same way he builds his understanding of the rest of the world: he uses the trial-and-error method. The child guesses what might be a part of his parent's worldview, and then he compares his guess with what he already knows about his parent to see if it fits. If it does fit, he assumes his guess was correct.

But we need to get more specific. I have broken the process down into three steps: gathering information, interpreting information, and determining principles. I will describe each one in detail.

Step 1: Gathering Information

The accuracy of the child's model will obviously depend on the amount of information he has to work with. Any child who spends much time around his parent has lots of information. I will describe the kinds of information that a child uses and compare those with the kinds of information we have that tell us about God's worldview.

One kind of information that a child can use is what his parents say. They give commands; they explain commands; they explain their own perspectives on things. Everything a parent says is generated by his worldview and therefore betrays that worldview. Therefore, what parents say is an important source of information the child can go to work on.

Another kind of helpful information is that which the child gains from observing his parent in action. This information can be particularly revealing. Let us say Johnny comes home from school and turns on the TV. His mother says, "You can't watch TV!" This appears to be clear enough, but why did Johnny's mother say it? Using her understanding of the world, she decided Johnny should not watch TV. But what, in her understanding of the world, forms a basis for this command? Observation may provide the necessary information. After Johnny leaves the room, his mother changes the channel and sits down to watch her favorite program. This piece of information does not tell Johnny why his mother forbade him to watch TV, but it does suggest a possibility that Johnny might have overlooked. So observation of the parent provides the child with helpful information.

Let us compare this with the information we have to build our theology. We lack direct information from God: we do not hear God give us commands and explanations; we do not observe His behavior day in and day out. But in the Bible we have a record of God's commands and instructions to other people and a description of some of His actions. Therefore, we have the opportunity to observe God in action just as

Johnny observes his parent, and we have commands and explanations given by God, although they were given to men who lived at another time.

The fact that the commands and explanations in the Bible were all directed to other people is not an insurmountable problem for us. We are capable of making the necessary adjustments. Johnny does this very thing. If he has mud all over his shoes just like his brother Billy does, and if he is standing right behind Billy when Mother tells Billy to wipe his feet before coming into the house, Johnny can figure out what to do. He interprets and analyzes the command to Billy as he does all information, but this kind of information is no less useful than any other. In theory, then, the fact that the Bible records commands and explanations directed to another immediate audience does not cause us any particular problem. In practice, however, interpreting this secondhand information is sometimes difficult. But it is difficult only because we lack supplementary information. A child has an enormous amount of information to work with; the Bible, by comparison, is frustratingly brief.

Another important source of information is experience. Johnny's parents have lived life awhile. They have bumped into reality a lot, and their worldview must take reality into account. Because Johnny experiences the same reality as his parents, he can use the information he gains from just living life to help him understand his parents' worldview.

An example is in order. We commanded our daughter not to touch the wood stove when she was little. It was not obvious to her why we gave the command. Did the wood stove fall into the same category as glass figurines—fragile, something she could easily break? Did it fit into the category of the TV—something she could get messy? Or did it fit into the category of a knife—something that could hurt her? These were all possibilities. But once she had touched the wood stove and had been burned, it was clear to which category the wood stove belonged. Without that experience, however, it was hard for her to know the rationale behind the command. We, her parents, had been burned by wood stoves before, and we gave our command to spare her. A parent's worldview is based partially on an experience of reality, and his commands originate from that worldview. A child experiences the same reality, and he can use the information he gains from this experience to help him understand the purposes behind those commands. Therefore, experience of reality is another good source of information.

A child can also learn from the experience of others. If my daughter had seen the stove burn someone else, she would have had enough information to conclude correctly why we commanded her not to touch it.

Experience of reality is also essential in the construction of a theology. (Remember, by *theology* I mean our model of God's understanding of reality.) The Bible is full of opportunities for me to learn from the experience of others. I do not have to kill my brother out of jealousy to know how God would respond; Cain did that. I do not have to betray my Lord to know what that would be like; Judas did that. Those experiences and many more are recorded in Scripture. Much of Scripture is history, and history is a record of the experience of others. We would do well to learn from what those before us have done.

Without a solid base of experience, I cannot generate a realistic view of the world. As servants of the God of truth, our perspective on reality should be realistic. To construct a theology in isolation from experience is to live in a fairyland. Therefore, our own experience and the experiences of others are important sources of data that we can use to build our theology.

Note, however, that the relationship between Johnny's parents and reality is different from the relationship between God and reality. Both Johnny and his parents are immersed in reality; therefore, they both have to take it into account. A parent cannot change the fact that a hot wood stove burns; he can only give commands that take this fact into account. Knowing this, a child then uses his knowledge of reality to help him understand the command. Reality is a given for both parents and children.

This is not true of God. Reality is the handiwork of God Himself. Because any creation tells much about the creator, it is to be expected that reality would tell us much about God. The natural order, operating as it does according to physical laws, tells us that God is a God of order. Reality, however, does not consist merely of physical laws. God did not create the world and the physical laws, then step back and renounce all responsibility for the ensuing events. Reality is still under construction: everything that happens is a foreseen and calculated result of God's activity. Therefore, if I should fall tomorrow and break my leg, reality has not gone amok; God tailor-made this situation for me. Everything that happens to me is the result of God personally interacting with me. So experience is an important source of information; it can tell me a great deal about God. But as with any piece of information, experience cannot contribute to our theology until we interpret it, which brings us to our next step.

Step 2: Interpreting Information

A child gathers information and then interprets it. *Every* bit of information must be interpreted. Even an explicit command that you might think could not be clearer can be misunderstood; the child must still put the command into the context of his parent's whole worldview. A true story will prove my point. When my nephew was young, his mother gave him the following command: "Put on a clean pair of underwear every day." About a week later, my nephew approached his mother and complained about stomach pains. His mother, with great medical acumen, felt his abdomen and deduced that the pains were caused by the seven pairs of underpants he was wearing. My nephew needed more information in order to understand what his mother wanted him to do. The point: verbal information is not foolproof. It can be, and often is, misunderstood. (Because the Bible is verbal information and therefore also susceptible to misinterpretation, much of this book describes the art of interpreting human language.)

Experience must also be interpreted. Just as the interpreter of language asks the question "What is the author saying?" so the interpreter of experience asks, "What is happening?" It may seem that experience does not need interpreting, because we usually interpret it so quickly that we are unaware of doing so. But we *do* interpret it.

Johnny comes home from a baseball game and tells his parents that he committed an error on the hit that scored the game-winning run. Following this announcement, his father walks out of the room without saying a word. For the most part, the facts are clear, but an important question is not resolved—what was Johnny's father's reaction? Was the father so embarrassed for his son that he could not look at him? Was the father so distracted with his own thoughts that he had not even heard Johnny, so that his departure was unrelated to the baseball incident? Johnny must accurately establish the nature of his father's reaction before he can use this information to determine what, if anything, the incident reveals about his father's values.

Building a theology also requires the interpretation of experience. Paul had to interpret his experience on the road to Damascus. Luke relayed the facts:

> As he was traveling, it happened that he was
> approaching Damascus, and suddenly a light from
> heaven flashed around him; and he fell to the
> ground and heard a voice saying to him, "Saul, Saul,
> why are you persecuting Me?" And he said, "Who
> are You, Lord?" And He said, "I am Jesus whom you

are persecuting, but get up and enter the city, and it will be told you what you must do." The men who traveled with him stood speechless, hearing the voice, but seeing no one. (Acts 9:3-7)

Was it a hallucination? Was it madness? Or was it Jesus? Paul decided it was really Jesus, but he had to interpret his experience.`

Information that has not been interpreted is useless. But interpreted information cannot be directly applied either. A coherence must be found in those interpretations. That is what we will take up next.

Step 3: Determining Principles

Interpreting a text is a matter of asking, "What?"; determining principles is a matter of asking, "Why?" A child assumes (perhaps gratuitously) that the parent's statements and actions come from a rational mind. Therefore, those actions and statements should manifest a degree of consistency. That consistency can be explained in terms of principles that the parent believes to be true. Principles, as I am using the word, are elements of a world-view. They can be descriptive ("the world is round," "people die," "ice cream tastes good") or prescriptive ("children should be seen and not heard," "laws ought not be violated," "do unto others . . . "). When all of these principles are put together into a coherent whole, the result is the parent's view of all of reality. Let us see how a determination of principles works.

If Johnny is commanded not to get his clothes dirty, he must determine why the command was given. He says to him-self, *Given all that I know about what Mama believes to be true, why would she give this command? It could be that she believes clothes should never get dirty. But that cannot be true: Mama gets her clothes dirty. It could be that I should not do anything knowingly to get my clothes dirty. But Papa does when he works on the car. It could be that only children should not knowingly get their clothes dirty.* . . . And so it goes until the child finds a line of reasoning that fits what he knows to be true about his parent's thinking. Eventually the child comes up with a list of values or principles that must be part of his parent's worldview, and he should be able to point to evidence that substantiates each one. It looks something like this:

1. Clothes are expensive. (Johnny learned this fact from experience and instruction.) And clothes should not be ruined needlessly. (He learned this value from his parent's instruction.)
2. Stains ruin clothes. (He learned from experience that clothes can be stained. He learned from instruction and observation of his parents that stained clothes are ruined clothes.) And dirt sometimes stains. (He learned this fact from personal experience.)
3. Old clothes can be worn when clothes are apt to get dirty. (His parents taught him this through instruction and example.)
4. One needs to be particularly careful with good clothes. (This is another learned value, closely related to numbers 1 and 3.)
5. Some accidents cannot be avoided. (He learned this from experience.) And good clothes will sometimes get dirty even if one is careful.
6. Some things are more important than keeping good clothes clean. (He learned this value from observing his parents.) And one thing more important than keeping clothes clean is the life of another person. Consequently, if his brother Joey is drowning, he should jump in and save Joey even if he (Johnny) has on good clothes.

These principles, then, are the child's best guess for why his mother commanded him not to get his clothes dirty. If Johnny is correct, then these are the principles that his mother believes to be true; each of the principles on the list above is part of her worldview.

The child compares each hypothesized set of principles with everything he has learned previously about his parent. The principles and values he thinks his parent holds should not contradict one another. Therefore, if Johnny stumbles upon two contradictory principles, he assumes he has not yet understood his parent correctly, and he needs to do more work. Behind every apparent contradiction there should be a deeper consistency. Therefore, Johnny determines how every new piece of information fits his model. If he finds any contradictions, he reworks something: either his model is wrong and needs to be altered or else he has misinterpreted his latest information. (A parent is capable of having an inconsistent worldview, but Johnny must not resort to this explanation of an apparent contradiction until all other possibilities have been explored thoroughly.) Thus, he constantly fine-tunes his model and makes it more comprehensive.

We do the same thing as we build our theology. We must determine the principles in God's worldview that account for every piece of information. In 1 Corinthians 9:9-10 Paul did a little determination of principles. He quoted Deuteronomy 25:4 ("You shall not muzzle the ox while he is threshing") and then posed the question "Why did God give this command?" First, he entertained the possibility that God gave it out of concern for the oxen. But he dismissed this. Then he asked if it could be for our sake. Bingo—that's it. God gave this command so that man would understand that a worker ought to be allowed to benefit from the fruit of his labor. This is the principle that explains why God gave the command.

As we attempt to understand God's worldview, we must draw principles from experience also. God is personally active in everything that happens. Therefore, it makes sense to ask for each event, "Why did this happen?" We may not be able to determine the rationale for every event, but we cannot doubt that it is consistent with God's worldview.

John recorded an incident in which Jesus helped the apostles draw a principle from their experience (John 9:1-3). Having encountered a man who had been blind from birth, the disciples asked Jesus whether the man was blind because of (A) his own sin or (B) his parents' sin. Jesus' answer was C, none of the above. The man was blind so that the works of God could be displayed in him. The disciples' guesses were not even close; Jesus had to help them understand the significance of their experience.

Often our experience is difficult to interpret. God does some things for reasons that are hard to figure out. My wife has had four miscarriages. Why? I do not know. All I know is that if I had more knowledge, it would all fit. However, I realize that in this life I may never get that kind of knowledge.

Fortunately, in one respect our task is a little neater than that of a child's. Whereas human beings can be inconsistent, God cannot be. And whereas parents can misunderstand reality, God cannot. Therefore, we should be even less tolerant of inconsistencies when we build a theology than a child is when he constructs a model of his parent's worldview. But because God is the transcendent Creator of the universe, we should not be surprised that many of His ways seem strange and mysterious.

When I claim that God's principles may be mysterious but not contradictory, *mystery* and *contradiction* may appear to be just two different words for the same thing. But they are actually very different concepts. A contradiction exists when two propositions are logically incompatible. A mystery exists when our limited experience makes two propositions seem unlikely both to be true. To say, for example, that a table exists and does not exist at the same time and in the same way is a contradiction. Only a rejection of logic itself could resolve these two propositions. That a solid table consists mostly of empty space and particles so small that they cannot be seen is a mystery. My experience makes it difficult to believe that a table can be solid and yet mostly empty space, but it is not a contradiction.

If Johnny persists in working to understand his parent's worldview and is on the lookout for the appearance of contradictions, his model will continually improve. If we are careful and persistent in trying to understand God's worldview, and if we are sensitive to contradictions, our understanding of truth will grow and improve.

The importance of this step cannot be overemphasized. Until the principles are extracted from a command (or any other piece of information), Johnny cannot act on it intelligently. A determination of principles makes it possible to release a command from a particular set of circumstances and allow it to inform actions in a completely different set of circumstances. I will talk about this more in the next chapter.

SOME IMPLICATIONS OF THE WORLDVIEW-BUILDING PROCESS

YOU CAN PROBABLY see that the process I have described has some important implications. I would like to make some of the most important ones explicit and comment on them.

1. Experience and Scripture both contribute to our theology. Before I began thinking about this process carefully, I thought Scripture was the only primary source of truth available to us. Therefore, if my understanding of Scripture ever came in conflict with my understanding of experience, then my understanding of experience had to be wrong. I still believe the Bible enjoys a unique authority vis-à-vis experience, but its uniqueness must be carefully understood.

Certainly the Bible is qualitatively different from our experience of reality. The Bible is expressed in words—a form of communication we understand. Experience, by contrast, is not propositional. The Bible instructs; experience does not. Therefore, the Bible is uniquely valuable. But experience is not without value. So although the kinds of information we get from the Bible and from experience are different, they are both reliable sources of data about the truth. God is the author of both the Bible and experience.

As I mentioned earlier, the Bible and experience are sources of information (raw data) and they are both susceptible to misunderstanding. They can be misinterpreted, and wrong principles can be drawn from them. The young businessman who looks around, sees that the wealthy are the ones who command respect and wield power, and decides on the basis of this observation that wealth is to be pursued at all costs has misunderstood experience. He is willing to sacrifice friends, family, personal integrity—in a word, his soul—to reach his goal. Such a person has misunderstood experience with disastrous consequences.

Because we have seen so many people misunderstand their experience, we Christians tend to be suspicious of experience itself. It is fair to conclude that we must be careful when we analyze experience, but we ought not conclude that experience itself is unreliable. Many people misapply the Bible, but do we assume that the cause is a defect in the Bible itself? Of course not. Therefore, when people misunderstand their experience, we should realize that the source of the problem lies not in the experience but in the interpretation of that experience.

Paul had great respect for the value of experience. His argument in the first chapter of Romans assumes that experience of reality is a source of information about the truth that is available to everyone. He said, "Since the creation of the world [God's] invisible attributes, His eternal power and divine nature, have been clearly seen, being understood through what has been made, so that they are without excuse" (Romans 1:20). There are two sources of information, then, for us to draw upon in our search for truth: Scripture and our experience of reality. Together, they work to help keep us on the right track. And as we shall see, we can use one to check our understanding of the other.

Sometimes the clear teaching of the Bible keeps us from a tempting but inaccurate understanding of experience. Let me give an example. Our society has reached the point where equality of the sexes is assumed. Society understands this to imply the rightness of an egalitarian marriage relationship. Experience does seem to demonstrate that women are just as intelligent and capable of leadership as men. If I were to look at experience alone, I would be persuaded of the soundness of egalitarian marriages. But there are passages in the Bible that teach male headship within marriage. Unless it can convincingly be shown that the Bible's teaching with respect to male headship is tied to the circumstances of the time, male headship must be upheld in spite of experience.

On the other hand, our experience is a check on our interpretation of Scripture. An example of this, too, is in order. In John 14:14 Jesus said, "If you ask Me anything in My name, I will do it." Let us interpret this passage to mean that Jesus will fulfill any request I make of Him in a prayer that I conclude with the words "In Jesus' name." If I pray that I will win the million-dollar sweepstakes, conclude my prayer with the obligatory "In Jesus' name," but do not win the sweepstakes, then I need to reconsider the initial interpretation. My experience of reality has made my interpretation of Scripture no longer tenable.

When our interpretation of reality does not match our understanding of Scripture, we should not conclude that Scripture is in error, nor should we conclude that reality is in error. Both Scripture and reality are accurate revelations from God; therefore, they must be consistent. If we find apparent discrepancies between Scripture and reality, then we have misunderstood something. Each is a check on the other. Together, experience and Scripture provide an adequate information base for constructing a trustworthy, realistic understanding of the basic components of God's worldview.

I should point out that experience of reality gives us information not found in the Bible. For instance, the Bible has little to say about gravity, inertia, kinetic energy, and centrifugal force. On the other hand, the Bible is an excellent source of information that I would never have known via experience alone. For example, if it were not for the Bible, I would never have known about salvation and redemption.

If you want to remove a screw, a wrench is worthless but a screwdriver is just the ticket. If you want to loosen a nut, a screwdriver is a bad choice but a wrench would do nicely. If, however, you want to remove a bolt held by a nut, you need no less than both the screwdriver and the wrench. Similarly, experience and Scripture are two entirely different resources. If I want to know how to be a good rhubarb farmer, I will get little help from the Bible. If I want to know how God has dealt with the problem of sin, experience is going to be of little value. But if I want to know how to be a good husband, I need to study both Scripture and experience.

2. Commands become outdated, but they are never irrelevant. We need to make a couple of observations about commands. A command is always addressed to a specific person or group of persons in a specific situation. Imagine a football team. The players are in the huddle when the quarterback turns to the split end and says, "Run a down-and-out." What if everyone on the team ran a down-and-out? The command was addressed to the split end. The quarterback had a particular purpose in mind when he gave this command, and his purpose did not include the whole team doing the same thing.

Imagine the same team, same game, ten plays later. Our heroes still (miraculously) have possession of the football. The quarterback calls a post pattern on this play, but the split end remembers the command he had received ten plays earlier to run a down-and-out and proceeds to obey that command on this play instead. The quarterback had given the command to run a down-and-out in response to a particular set of circumstances, but ten plays later the circumstances have changed and that command is outdated.

Two observations need to be underscored. First, a speaker gives commands to a specific individual or individuals. The command may be given to one person or eight billion people, but the speaker has a specific target group in mind. Second, a command is addressed to a specific set of circumstances, and it is valid only as long as there is no significant change in the circumstances. That is, the command is valid only as long as there has been no change that negates the original purpose of the command.

When my daughter was younger, I insisted that she not touch the television set. I had a couple of concerns. She did not know what parts of the television were safe to touch and what parts were not; therefore, I thought it best that she not touch the television at all. My other concern was for the television. When she was younger, her hands were always coated with the primordial goo endemic to toddlers; if she were to touch the television set, she would just mess it up.

I did not intend that my wife obey the command I gave my daughter. My wife keeps her hands clean, and she knows what parts of a television might be dangerous. My wife is not the one to whom I addressed my command, because the reasons that I gave the command to my daughter did not apply to my wife. If my daughter had a twin brother, however, the brother would be well advised to obey the command as well. The reasons I had for telling my daughter not to touch the television would apply also to him.

Now my daughter is older, and I have been known to ask her to turn on the television. How could I do such a thing? Because she now knows which parts of the set she can touch and which ones she cannot, and she keeps her hands relatively clean. In other words, the situation has changed such that the command is no longer needed. However, the principles that produced the original prohibition are still part of my worldview: (1) I do not want anyone to get hurt; and (2) I do not want the television to be covered with goo.

This is all-important when we consider the commands we find in Scripture. We must realize that none of the Bible was explicitly written to us. For example, I do not know that any of the authors of Scripture envisioned me as a member of his reading audience, and consequently I cannot assume that any of Scripture's commands were given to me. While it is true that, in a sense, God intended the Bible to be a communication to all of mankind, it is the human author's intent that is accessible to us and therefore the one we are trying to discover. In the absence of any explicit evidence that a given passage of the Bible was written to me, I must assume that it was written to a more immediate audience. Taken at face value, therefore, all the commands in Scripture were addressed to people who are long since dead and gone. We ought not thoughtlessly follow commands given to others.

This does not mean, however, that the commands in Scripture are irrelevant to us. We are just forced to do some work. The command must be interpreted, and the principles that produced the command must be determined. Notice that this is the procedure we need to use to process all information about God's worldview. Accordingly, every command that God proclaims to someone is just more information about God's perspective on reality.

Let me illustrate how I am suggesting we deal with the commands in Scripture. God commanded the male descendants of Abraham to be circumcised. And yet Paul made it clear in his letter to the Galatians that they were not to be circumcised. God gave the command to Abraham for a reason. Circumcision was intended to be a visible, permanent symbol in recognition of God's relationship to His people. It was intended to call to mind God's graciousness in the past and

His commitment to carry out His promises for the future. Such a symbol was no longer appropriate for Gentile Christians. In fact, circumcision had come to have a very different significance in Galatia—one that was contrary to the gospel. In the light of that significance, circumcision would be wrong. But the original intent of the symbol—to remind God's people of His graciousness and loyalty to His promises—remains valid. Our gratitude and concomitant trust in Him will never be outdated.

God also commanded the Israelites not to commit adultery (Exodus 20:14). Am I obligated to follow this command? I would say yes. But I have to go through a number of steps to reach this conclusion: (1) The command is best understood as a law established to preserve the sanctity of marriage, which God Himself instituted. (2) The principle that adultery undermines marriage and therefore ought not be committed now becomes part of my theology. (3) I can then apply my theology: God's purpose for the law against adultery will not be done away with until marriage itself ceases to be; therefore, I should not commit adultery. As it turns out, I conclude that I am obligated to obey this command. But because it was not addressed directly to me, I had to go through a series of steps to establish this.

3. God's worldview contains a hierarchy of principles. From God's perspective, some things are more important than other things. It is important for us to determine the value that He has assigned to each. An example will demonstrate what I mean. I could tell my daughter that I do not want her to break the window, my reason being that I do not approve of the destruction of property. As a general rule, there is no good reason to break the window. But if there were a fire, and if my daughter broke the window to escape, I would commend her action. My daughter's life is worth any number of windows. I want her to understand that I value her life above the value of the window. I expect her to interpret my command in the context of my values; this is a part of my worldview.

As a parent, I do not want mechanical, unthinking obedience from my daughter. I want her to adopt my worldview for her own. I want her to agree with and embrace my values and principles and live accordingly (even when I am not looking). I call this mature obedience.

God wants the same thing from us; He just uses different words to describe it. Matthew 12:1-8 records an incident in which the disciples were criticized by the Pharisees for plucking and eating grain on the Sabbath. Jesus defended His friends by reminding the Pharisees that, even though the law forbade it, David and his comrades ate the showbread without blame because they were desperate for food. Jesus also pointed out that the priests violated the Sabbath law in the course of their regular duties and were not held culpable. He concluded by saying, "If you had known what this means, 'I desire compassion, and not a sacrifice,' you would not have condemned the innocent" (verse 7). By this Jesus was claiming that God wants our actions to be motivated by a love for Him and loyalty to His standard of right and wrong. He does not want mechanical, self-serving compliance.

4. Integrity is the only escape from a bad theology. We have a worldview before we even begin to read Scripture. It's a worldview that affects both our interpreting of texts and our determining of principles. What is more, we expect (and therefore tend to find) interpretations and principles that are consistent with our worldview. We reinforce our initial beliefs. If Scripture is to inform our thinking, we must be sensitive to apparent contradictions. They signal the possibility that we need to change our worldview in some respect in order to conform to God's worldview. We must respond to this signal and follow the evidence wherever it leads. This is integrity. We must have good reasons for what we believe to be true, and when we have no good evidence, we must admit that we are speculating. This kind of brutal honesty with ourselves and others is our only hope. Otherwise, we are not being instructed by Scripture; we are just toying with it.

5. Building a reliable theology is a lifelong process. To make God's worldview our own is literally a superhuman task. I do not even know my parents' worldview in detail; I know it only in its broad outline. And while my parents are smart, they do not know as much as God. God knows everything. Therefore, to know God's worldview in its broadest outline is the best we can hope for in this life.

Fortunately, not everything is equally urgent. For me to know that salvation from sin is by faith is much more important than knowing the chemical makeup of camel spit (I hear it's great for defogging glasses). No man will ever know all of truth in this life. In practice, therefore, our goal is to learn as much of God's perspective as we can, starting with the most important truths and working from there.

It is hard work. The amount of data is overwhelming, and although we will work on it all our lives, we will not be done when we die. But do not let this stop you. Our assignment here on earth is to live a righteous life. How can we know what it means to live a righteous life if we do not know what God requires of us? I could spend hundreds of hours standing on my head in a bed of razor blades chanting without pause, but if God does not want me to do it, then I have labored in vain. My action is not obedient unless God asks me to do it. Therefore, we must know what God wants us to do. Then, by the grace of God, we will someday hear Him say, "Well done, good and faithful servant."

6. Humility is important in worldview building. We are all aware that we make mistakes. When it comes to theology and doctrine, we can err, too. To admit to an error and make the proper changes is better than to insist that we are correct. Humility is an important ally. Without it we cannot learn. We must be humble before our fellow men as well as before God; we need their help and His. Only if we are humble will we be able to avail ourselves of their help.

A correct understanding of what is true is vitally important. But a correct understanding is not the most important
thing in life; no one will make it into heaven on the basis of
sound doctrine. If I could give you only one of two gifts—
a knowledge of all that is true or an unshakable confidence
that God loves you and has your best interests in mind—I
would want you to have the latter. Only it brings eternal life.
Knowledge is nice, but it is way down on the list of things
most important in life. We must keep this in perspective. We
should not fight for what we believe to be true while tram-
pling a brother under foot. Paul said, "If I . . . know all mysteries and all knowledge . . . , but do not have love, I am
nothing" (1 Corinthians 13:2).

WORLDVIEW STUDY: JAMES 5:13-16

I WILL GRANT that what I have said in this chapter makes
understanding the Scriptures sound more difficult than you
may have previously thought. Our task would be much easier if we could just read the instructions in Scripture and do
them. But the Bible was not written that way. The Bible is a
record of God's dealings with man. Commands in Scripture
are examples of God's worldview applied to concrete situations that we are not personally a part of. We have no choice—
we must treat Scripture as information that has to be
interpreted. It is God's will for us to try to understand His
worldview and act in accordance with it. Principle upon principle, value upon value, we slowly reconstruct in our own
minds God's worldview—truth. Every passage of Scripture in
some way makes a contribution to this end.

So far, I have talked only about how we construct a model
of God's worldview. I have yet to talk about how we apply that
worldview. That will be the topic of the next chapter. Before

we get there, however, I want to illustrate how we can analyze a passage and use it to help construct the worldview. Let us return to the now-familiar passage in James 5:13-20 to see how it can contribute to the cause.

A Brief Statement of Interpretation

In this book my fellow authors and I have not fully developed and defended an interpretation of the James passage. Nor can I do that here. We have produced such a commentary and placed it on our Web site.[1] For the purposes of this chapter, I will briefly summarize the import of these verses.

James was writing to believers who were being persecuted because of their faith—a persecution most acutely felt in the pocketbook. They were greatly tempted to act in an ungodly manner in order to lessen their suffering, which could mean anything from yielding to a rich man a highly prized, front-row seat (in our churches it would be a highly prized, back-row seat) to abandoning the faith. As the persecution persisted, it became increasingly difficult for them to continue to trust that God did indeed love them, that their suffering was indeed the best thing for them. Consequently, some among the believers struggled to maintain their faith. They were weak in faith, but they did not want to turn their backs on Christianity and walk away from God. What could they do? How could they be helped?

James told these people that they should call the elders—the leaders of the church, people who were spiritually mature. The elders were to go to the one struggling and pray with him, presumably helping him to request forgiveness and spiritual strength. The elders were also to anoint the petitioner with oil in order to express in a physical symbol what was happening at a spiritual level. James told the people that if a person struggling with his faith did this, recognizing his need and asking for forgiveness, God would help him. God would forgive the sins committed out of faithlessness and would strengthen the person's faith.

Principles Behind the Command

Now we need to list the principles that explain this command. I will not list all of the principles behind James' command to call the elders (5:14). A complete list would be very long because I would have to drag out most of a full-blown view of reality. For example, one principle that must have been a part of James' thinking was this: God exists. This principle, however, is just one of James' foundational beliefs, which were far removed from the command itself. I will not list these foundational beliefs, because they are numerous and because I hope they have been well established already on the basis of other evidence. Similarly, I did not list such foundational beliefs in the example of Johnny's thinking about his mother's command. Clearly, a child believes that his parent exists and that he, the child, exists. Otherwise, there would be no command. Such foundational principles need not be examined unless a given bit of information appears to contradict one of those principles. To the extent that these foundational principles are well substantiated and harmonious with the information we are processing, we can concentrate on other aspects of God's worldview. We must never forget, however, that even these principles could be in error, and we must be willing to reexamine them. For now, let us move on to the principles directly behind James' command.

What principles are most closely related to James' command? That is, for what principles could I use this passage as a proof text (in the good sense of the term)? We need to reconstruct an outline of the logic James used to arrive at his decision to give the command. I would outline his thinking as follows:

1. God comes to the aid of the repentant.
2. One who wants help in his struggle against his faithlessness is repentant of that faithlessness.
3. Faithlessness is ultimately a reluctance or refusal to accept what is true.

4. The best antidote for faithlessness is a clear understanding of God's perspective on things.
5. Wise believers have the best understanding of God's
perspective on things.
6. God likes to use people as instruments of His ministry.
7. Physical symbols (such as the oil) can help people
understand what is happening spiritually.

The Contribution Made by the Principles

Here is how these principles contribute to James' advice. James
had noticed that some of the believers were so distraught about
their situation that they were on the verge of complete despair.
They were having trouble believing that God was taking care
of those who trusted Him. James knew that God is committed
to perfecting those who trust Him. Therefore, he wanted to
reassure those who were wavering of God's commitment to
them. His advice is very practical. He told those who were
struggling that they should summon the elders, because the
elders were wise, mature believers who understood the pressures and the temptations to doubt and yet were convinced of
God's love and control of the situation. They would be able
to counsel, encourage, and sympathize with the beleaguered
brother. This was in keeping with God's clear preference for
using people to carry out His purposes. James encouraged
them to entreat God to replace the doubting with faith and to
ask God for forgiveness of sins resulting from the lack of faith.
Because physical symbols can aid people's understanding of
what is happening at the spiritual level, James recommended
a ceremony that graphically represented God's forgiveness and
aid. James followed this with an exhortation to continual con-
fession and prayer, as proof of trust in God's ability and willingness to do what He purposes.

Did all of these principles come solely from this passage? Not exactly. I drew upon my understanding of God's
worldview in order to explain the command in a way that

is consistent with it. So then, I see the principles in this passage through the grid of my understanding of God's worldview. I have tried to reconstruct James' thinking in a way that does not violate my interpretation of the text or deviate from my understanding of God's worldview. If I were to have any difficulty reconciling my interpretation with my understanding of God's worldview, then I would have to find the cause of the disharmony and make the appropriate change. This adjustment would probably create ripples that would affect other parts of my theology. But until I run into a contradiction or have some other reason to believe that my understanding of truth is wrong, I will maintain my present beliefs.

Why Applications Differ

You have probably had an experience in which, while you agreed with someone else about the *interpretation* of a given verse, you significantly disagreed with him about the *application* of the verse. There are two possible causes for this.

The interpretations differ. Sometimes the apparent agreement on the interpretation is, in fact, only superficial. Let us say I am discussing the James passage with someone. We have compared notes on our interpretations of the passage, and we agree on every point. But when we begin to discuss how the principles ought to be applied, my interlocutor is particularly insistent that elders be called in order for the prayer of spiritual strengthening to take place. I agree that the elders ought to be called, but I do not consider it crucial. Why the difference in emphasis?

As we investigate the matter more thoroughly, we discover that we understood the word *elder* differently. My interlocutor has understood the word to refer to an office. Unless the one who is called is a current member of the Board of Elders in our church, we will not be following the teaching of James on this issue. I, on the other hand, have understood the word *elder* to refer to a wise and mature believer. In this meaning of the word it would not matter if the one called held any office at all.

As it turns out, then, our difference in emphasis was due to a difference in interpretation. We did not see it at first; it became apparent only as a result of further discussion and investigation. But it was there all along.

The theologies differ. The other cause could be a difference in theology. For instance, someone could argue that the anointing ceremony is an integral part of what James was commanding; God sees the physical symbolism as so important that He prescribes it. The interpretation I have offered does not negate this possibility. A disagreement such as this cannot be resolved on the basis of James 5:13-16 alone. The disagreement is due to differences that existed in our theologies before we even turned to James 5. Because James 5 said nothing to challenge this point, both parties were able to retain their former perspectives. Therefore, to resolve this difference, other evidence from the Bible and experience would have to be introduced into the discussion.

In practice it is sometimes difficult to resolve these differences. Egos get in the way; emotion and psychological commitments cloud reason; people have different amounts of wisdom. There are many obstacles to reaching a consensus that corresponds to the truth. But patience and humility, resulting in a willingness to listen carefully to the other person, will produce a mutual understanding, if not agreement.

However, an understanding of the method we use to construct our theology is helpful in resolving differences. By making explicit all of the thinking that is behind a given theological conclusion, both parties can examine each step to see if there are any mistakes. If the whole process is left at the intuitive level, there can be no basis for discussion.

Agreement, of course, is not the goal. Coming to know the truth is the goal. God works in strange and wonderful ways to shape our knowledge of the truth. He often takes us through a series of experiences that make clear an element of the truth that was not previously a part of our theology. I do not know how many times I have rejected a theological conclusion, only to reach that same conclusion in subsequent years. The truth is complicated and extensive. It takes a lot of Bible study, experience, and reflection to understand it.

Real progress can be made. We interpret passages, draw principles from them, and build our theology. As contradictions and difficulties become apparent, we deal with them. Slowly but surely, our theology improves. A sound theology—an accurate model of God's worldview—is the goal of Bible study.

STUDY QUESTIONS

1. You have given your child a rule that he cannot cross the street without holding the hand of an adult. Under what circumstances would you allow your child to violate this rule? Why?

   a. The road has been closed due to snow.

   b. The road is closed for repaving.

   c. The child has turned twenty-one.

   d. There is an earthquake, and the only place where building debris is not falling is in the street.

   e. A pedestrian overpass has been built.

   f. The road has been permanently closed and traffic rerouted.

   g. The child has turned ten.

   How would these exceptions to the rule be communicated to the child?

2. According to the perspective I have presented, we must apply a whole worldview rather than individual verses.

Read the exchange between Jesus and the Pharisees in Matthew 19:3-9 and analyze it in this regard.

3. In order to know the principle(s) behind a specific command, we must know why the command was given. For instance, what if we do not know why we were commanded to take communion or be baptized? Ought we participate in these ceremonies even if we do not know why we have been asked to do it?

4. How does one determine which commands are valid for all time and which are only temporarily valid?

5. Does this approach make morality relative to time and culture?

CHAPTER SEVEN

Applying God's Worldview

The moment Alice appeared, she was appealed to by all three to settle the question, and they repeated their arguments to her, though, as they all spoke at once, she found it very hard indeed to make out exactly what they said.

The executioner's argument was that you couldn't cut off a head unless there was a body to cut it off from: that he had never had to do such a thing before, and he wasn't going to begin at *his* time of life.

The King's argument was, that anything that had a head could be beheaded, and that you weren't to talk nonsense.

The Queen's argument was, that if something wasn't done about it in less than no time, she'd have everybody executed, all round.

LET ME REMIND YOU of the task we set for ourselves at the beginning of the previous chapter. We observed that the Bible consists of information written to people who lived at another time and in another place and are long since dead. When we interpret Scripture, we merely recover the meaning of what the human author wrote to his immediate audience. But what we want from the Bible is divine guidance in our day-to-day problems. In these two chapters I set out to bridge this gap between what we find in the Bible (interpretation) and what we need to know to lead godly lives (application).

What I have outlined up to this point is how to construct a model of God's understanding of all reality. I have called this model our "theology." Once we have constructed a reliable theology, we are able to predict what God would advise us to do in everyday situations. We are able to step into God's head and see any situation through His eyes. God's view of reality is transcultural; it can be applied to any time and place. It can even be brought to bear on the questions you face. In this chapter I will explain how to apply God's worldview once we have constructed our theology.

THE DECISION-MAKING PROCESS

THE APPLICATION OF God's worldview most commonly means deciding what to do in a particular situation. For instance, if I were laid off from work, I would have to decide what to do. Should I apply for unemployment benefits? Should I rob a bank? Should I spend all our savings on the lottery? Should I look for work where I live, or should we move? Should my wife look for work? There are a whole series of decisions my wife and I would have to make. Some of my options would be unrighteous; others would be righteous. Some would be wise; others would be unwise. How should I decide what God wants me to do in this situation?

How does the typical man on the street make decisions? He simply looks at the situation through his own worldview and chooses the option that most appeals to him. This often happens so quickly that he is completely unaware of what he is doing. But the process is actually very complex. As he looks at the situation, he immediately gives every factor its appropriate importance. His worldview instantaneously assigns a value to his personal comfort, to the welfare of his family, to the importance of money. Only very difficult decisions force him to think consciously about the relative importance of such things. His sense of right and wrong automatically eliminates those options that are contrary to his worldview. Much of this occurs without the person's conscious awareness.

The result of this process is a course of action that seems to be the best option. This is the decision. The person may not even be able to explain why this option is better than all the others. He only knows that when the situation is seen through his worldview it stands out as the preferable one.

There is nothing wrong with this approach to decision making. People are good at making decisions in keeping with their own worldviews. In fact, we all know that what a person does is a much more reliable guide to determining his true values and beliefs than what he says. So if we were perfect people who fully embraced God's worldview and made decisions accordingly, there would be no problem; all our decisions would be righteous. We would live life in perfect obedience to God. But this is not the case.

As Christians, we are committed in principle to God's worldview. We know we should adopt His worldview as our own, and we want to. However, we find part of ourselves still drawn to our previous, sinful worldview. As a result, we drift back and forth between worldviews without realizing it. As we evaluate a particular situation, some of the values we assign are from God's worldview and some are from our previous worldview. Our decisions, therefore, are sometimes righteous and sometimes not, depending on how uncompromisingly we have viewed the situation through God's eyes.

God is committed to perfecting us. He wants to instill in us a love for Him and His way of looking at the world. One day we will automatically live according to His worldview, but that day will not arrive in this lifetime. In this life we can expect only partial success. Nevertheless, we should strive to live truly godly lives. This is not easy. We have to acknowledge the rebellion within us and its subversion of our commitment to God's worldview. Our sinful nature constantly tries to pawn off ungodly values and beliefs as righteous ones. We must always be on guard for this. Therefore, although a Christian uses the same decision-making process as anyone else, he must fight his tendency to make the decision based on his natural, worldly perspective and strive to evaluate his options based on God's worldview.

The decision-making process is complex. I am not even going to try to describe it. Like any skill, it is not easily reduced to words without losing a great deal in translation. However, in recognition of the fact that our sinfulness is constantly trying to corrupt the decision-making process, I offer the following three questions as a means of helping us be honest with ourselves.

Question 1: Is This Action Inherently Sinful?

If the chosen course of action is inherently evil, then the decision is a bad one and should be rejected. The first check, then, is to reject any decision that is inherently wrong.

Some actions are wrong under any circumstances whatsoever. For instance, murder is always wrong. God gives life to each individual person, and He has given to no one the right to terminate that life. Therefore, it would never be possible to murder righteously. Murder is explicitly proscribed in the Bible. God's perspective on human life led Him to give a command to the Israelites through Moses that forbade them from committing murder: "You shall not murder" (Exodus 20:13). Because there is no reason to think that God's view of the sanctity of human life should be any different in our day, murder remains wrong. In fact, murder will always be an unrighteous act—no matter what the circumstances. The first test will always remove such an option.

Other actions are wrong under some circumstances but not others. The trick in this case is determining which kind of situation you are facing. My wife and I have thought a great deal about how to educate our children. One issue we face is whether we can send them to the public schools; is this a righteous option? I think every Christian would agree that under some circumstances it is perfectly legitimate to send one's children to a public school. On the other hand, every Christian would agree that it is possible for a public school to become such a hostile environment that no Christian parent should send his children there. But these are theoretical extremes. My wife and I must make a determination about a particular school: we must judge whether it is wrong to send our children to the school down the street. This school is not one of the extreme cases; it merely reflects society's increasingly hostile attitude toward Christianity. Has it crossed the line? Would it necessarily be wrong for us to send our children there? This is typical of the judgments we have to make in order to determine right and wrong action. We are often forced to beg God for greater wisdom in the face of such questions.

If we determine that the preferred course of action is not inherently wrong, then we cannot simply assume that it is the best possible course of action. Another question must be answered to determine this.

Question 2: Is This Action Unwise?

There are actions that are not inherently evil but are nevertheless unwise. Unwise actions are actions that demonstrate insufficient attention to the world around us. God created the world to operate in an orderly fashion. We can observe that order and learn to predict future events to a certain extent. For instance, everyone has noticed that when a rock is dropped it falls toward earth. If someone failed to acknowledge the existence of gravity and designed a piggy bank that used centrifugal force to load coins into the bank, we would call that foolish but we would not call it immoral. It is not inherently wrong to spend time devising any excessively complicated piggy bank; it is just silly.

Many actions fall into this category. Some of them are insignificant, such as drinking coffee. Some scientific research studies have found coffee drinking to be detrimental to one's health. Is it wrong to drink coffee? No. Is it unwise? Possibly. But other questions of wise or unwise action are matters of enormous consequence. When we vote for political candidates, we often must choose either a candidate with whom we agree on the issues but who is not of good character or else a candidate with whom we disagree on the issues but who is of good character. Is it wiser to vote on the basis of character or issues? This is a decision of great significance.

It is therefore prudent to reflect, "Is this action unwise?" We ought to learn about the world around us. We need to learn how the natural world operates; we need to learn how human beings operate; we need to learn about ourselves. The better our understanding of these things, the greater our wisdom will be. Making unwise decisions is not unrighteous, but sooner or later you will suffer for it.

Any action that is neither unrighteous nor unwise is a sound decision, so it would seem that no further questions are necessary. But there is one more question that ought to be asked.

Question 3: Is This Action Motivated by Evil?

No one ever does anything he considers truly wrong. The thief is justified by the wealth of his victim, the bomber is justified by the revolution, and the murderer denies he did it. We all want to feel that we have done right; therefore, we are willing to distort morality or even facts to justify our actions. So it may seem silly to include the step of questioning whether our preference is motivated by evil.

Christians are the only people in the world who have a realistic appreciation of the insidious nature of the sin within us. I am convinced that the best sign that a Christian is maturing is when he finds sin lurking in an area of his life he previously thought was pure. The better we understand the nature of righteousness, the better we recognize the sin in our own lives.

Sin is so devious that it can distort facts, values, and judgments without our conscious knowledge in order to justify its preferred action. In other words, because we are sinners, we are capable of convincing ourselves that an evil action is neither inherently wrong nor unwise. This is called rationalization. It is not a result of ignorance; it is a deliberate (even if subconscious) manipulation of facts and principles to make an otherwise sinful act seem righteous.

Because we are aware of the wicked and deceitful heart within us, it is only prudent to check our decision once more before we act on it. We stop and ask ourselves, *Why do I prefer this action?* Then we peer into our souls to see if we can identify any evil motivation: *Am I just fooling myself?* This check will not detect ignorance, only self-deception.

This check works like this: Joe has a son, Don, who has great athletic potential. Joe wants Don to play soccer on a local team. Don does not want to. Should Joe insist that Don play? Nothing is inherently wrong with this, and Joe has judged that it is not unwise. His preferred action has passed the first two checks. Now he must subject it to the last check.

In answer to the question "Why do you prefer this course of action?" Joe says he wants Don to play so that he will learn discipline and teamwork. These are indeed good things. If Joe has correctly assessed the situation, and if he is indeed trying to do what is best for Don, then he should insist on Don's athletic participation. But if Joe is actually motivated by a desire for vicarious stardom, then he stands convicted of seeking to do evil. He is seeking his own perceived best interests at the expense of his son's best interests.

If Joe detects an evil motive within himself, then the validity of all of the previous examination is called into question because his evil desire may have subtly distorted the process. Having judged his motive as evil, Joe must now go through the whole process again. Now, in light of his discovery, he may prefer a different action or he may still prefer the same action. In either case the choice must be submitted to the same three checks as all other decisions. It may be that Joe will end up preferring the same action, but this time he will assess it without the distortion present the first time.

Analyzing one's motives is difficult and wearisome. We all realize that we are very good at deceiving ourselves. So when we try to determine our real motives, we never know when we have found them. There is always a possibility that we are still deceiving ourselves. As a result, we can never know for certain what our motivations are for any action. We cannot, however, afford to be paralyzed by our introspection. Decisions have to be made. All we can do is be as honest with ourselves as possible and proceed accordingly.

Aspects of Decision Making

THE ACTUAL PROCESS Christians use to make decisions is no different from what others do; everyone looks at a situation and assesses it from the perspective of his own worldview. When a person becomes a Christian, he is choosing to embrace God's worldview as his own. A Christian will choose to act differently from a nonChristian not because he uses a different decision-making process but because he uses different values and principles to assess the circumstances. Our decisions will be righteous to the extent that we correctly understand and implement God's worldview. We will understand God's worldview only if we have a good grasp of the teaching of Scripture. This is why Bible study is worth all the effort.

A number of observations are worthy of separate treatment in light of this discussion:

God's Worldview
It is important to understand that determination of the rightness or wrongness of a given action is made on the basis of God's worldview, not on specific verses in the Bible. Some acts that are explicitly forbidden in the Bible are not forbidden by God's worldview under other circumstances, while other acts that are not explicitly forbidden in the Bible are forbidden by God's

worldview under some or even all circumstances.

The dietary laws are an example of the former. Based on Leviticus 11, which describes what foods the Israelites were allowed or forbidden to eat, we might conclude that God never wanted man to eat any of those foods that He labeled unclean. But this is not true. Jesus said, "'Do you not understand that whatever goes into the man from outside cannot defile him; because it does not go into his heart, but into his stomach, and is eliminated?' (Thus He declared all foods clean.)" (Mark 7:18-19). Jesus was saying that the foods God had declared to be unclean, and therefore not to be eaten by the Israelites, were suitable for consumption. On the basis of our theology (as I am using the word), we must determine the reason for this change. What had changed between the time the command was given and the time of Peter's dream that made the dietary laws inoperative?

Many of the laws given to the Israelites were didactic, designed to teach the Israelites spiritual principles that would be repeated and made clearer in the course of history. Just as a child learns to add and subtract using blocks but later abandons the blocks and moves on to more abstract concepts, so God employed religious ritual as a visual aid to teach spiritual truths. The food laws were this kind of visual aid, demonstrating the sharply defined distinction between clean and unclean. Every time the Israelites ate a meal, they were reminded of this distinction: what is clean is clean and what is unclean is unclean; there is no gray zone. They were to realize that the laws pertaining to ritual cleanness and uncleanness were helpful in understanding the concept of moral cleanness and uncleanness. Moral uncleanness is abhorrent to God, but He delights in moral cleanness. Furthermore, the difference between the morally clean and the morally unclean is sharply defined; there are no intermediate categories.

When Christ came, He did away with the need for the object lesson. Christ *was* moral cleanness, and His death made it possible for that which was morally unclean (sinful man) to become morally clean. The dietary laws and the other ritual distinctions between clean and unclean were no longer needed. Peter came to understand this in the course of the next few days: "He said to them [a group of Gentiles], 'You yourselves know how unlawful it is for a man who is a Jew to associate with a foreigner or to visit him; and yet God has shown me that I should not call any man unholy or unclean'" (Acts 10:28). The dietary laws, therefore, have served their purpose and God no longer requires them.

Now let us look at an example of an act that is clearly wrong according to God's worldview even though it is not explicitly proscribed in Scripture. God's worldview condemns having bare, electrical wiring in one's house such that a visitor could easily suffer serious harm from it. God wants us to take all reasonable precautions to protect people from harm while on our property or while using our possessions. This principle is taught in Deuteronomy 22:8: "When you build a new house, you shall make a parapet for your roof, so that you will not bring bloodguilt on your house if anyone falls from it." This verse commanded the Israelites to build a railing around their roof, which they used as part of the living space, so that no one would fall off and hurt himself. The principle behind this command is that God wants people to take all reasonable measures to make their property safe. This is merely a corollary of the more general principle of respect for human life. I know from experience that if someone touches bare, live electrical wiring, he can be seriously injured. When these two elements of God's worldview are combined, His worldview clearly condemns leaving exposed electrical wiring unprotected such that a visitor might easily get hurt, even though the Bible never mentions electricity.

It is important, therefore, to recognize that we are looking to our theology to determine whether a given action is righteous or not; we are not simply looking at specific verses in

Scripture. Our theology is the product of our examination of the Bible. If our theology has been carefully constructed, it should be wholly biblical. A sound theology corresponds exactly to God's worldview, and God's worldview is wholly biblical.

Cost/Benefit Analysis

To determine whether an action is wise or unwise can be difficult. Often we need to see if the good that will come from the act outweighs the bad. This can be better illustrated than explained.

My daughter has a condition called "lazy eye." Her eyes do not track together, so she sees double images. To deal with these double images, her brain stopped registering the image received by one eye. The doctor said this condition could be almost entirely corrected, but part of the treatment was to keep her "good" eye covered at all times for three months. If we did not carry through with the treatment, her vision in the one eye would be permanently impaired.

To have your eye covered for three months is not fun. My daughter could not see well (remember, the good eye was covered). The skin under the patch got hot and began to sweat. The standing sweat irritated the skin, making it painful to change old patches. It was a lot to put a young child through.

This is one of the many situations where a value judgment had to be made. There is nothing evil about having a child wear an eye patch. Nor is it evil to keep a child from wearing an eye patch. But there are costs and benefits to both actions. As parents, we had to calculate those benefits and costs to decide whether to go through with the treatment. If we went ahead with the treatment, our daughter would suffer three months of discomfort and inconvenience. That is a definite cost. On the other hand, she stood to gain near normal vision for the rest of her life. Did the benefit outweigh the cost?

In my daughter's case the answer was easy. But what if a child had a fatal illness for which a risky operation could only

204 | The Language of God

forestall the inevitable? Now do the benefits outweigh the costs? As you can see, these questions can get extremely difficult. Weighing the costs and benefits can be almost impossible. I call this a check for unwise actions because it takes a great deal of wisdom to make such determinations. We need wisdom at every step of the process from interpretation to application, but we need it particularly in the cost/benefit analysis.

As with every other part of the process, the cost/benefit analysis must be based on our theology, which (to the best of our knowledge) includes a list of everything God values, in order of importance. When we compare what will be lost with what will be gained by a given action, we must use God's values. If I am going to sell my house, I will be able to sell it for more if I do not tell the prospective buyers that the basement floods every winter. If dollars are the most important consideration, then I ought not mention the flooding. But if personal integrity is more important than the money, then wisdom dictates that I should tell the buyer about the flooding. So the standard of values we use makes an enormous difference in the outcome. We must use God's values if we are to end up with a righteous course of action.

Personal Preference
Whenever we are faced with a decision, we naturally gravitate toward taking the action we prefer. If I want to know whether the local bookstore has a particular book, my inclination is to go to the store to find out. My wife, on the other hand, is more likely to pick up the phone and call. Why? The phone is more convenient, so she uses it. But I dislike talking to people over the phone, so I am willing to take the less convenient route. It is a matter of personal preference. I cannot pinpoint the sources of my preferences; I can only make the general statement that they are the product of my personality and experience. Because God is the author of both our personality and our experience, He is the author of our personal

preferences. God has given us each a unique personality, which means we each have a unique set of preferences.

If two Christians go to the store and one buys a red shirt and the other buys a green shirt, neither has made the more righteous choice. They are simply expressing, in a small way, the uniqueness God built into each of them. When small differences like this are multiplied time and again, we begin to see personality. Nothing is wrong with this kind of variety among Christians. In this sense no one personality is more righteous than another.

When the issue of decision making is raised in Christian circles, the advice usually given is to think of what Christ would do. The impetus for this advice is certainly sound. Christ lived His life in perfect conformity to God's worldview. In that sense He is an excellent model. In practice, however, I have had difficulty operating on this advice. First, I do not have a complete picture of Jesus as a person. I sometimes try to picture what my father would do in various situations. In many instances I can, but there are many situations in which I have difficulty projecting how he would have acted. This is relevant because I know far more about my father as a person than I can glean from the Bible about Jesus. If I have trouble predicting what my father would do in some situations, then how much greater is the difficulty with respect to Jesus? A second problem with this device is that Jesus never was a father or a husband, so I have trouble visualizing what He would have done in certain fatherly or husbandly situations. The third problem—and the reason I raise this issue now—is that Jesus was another person. A person's personal preferences come into play as one makes various decisions. To act as Jesus did would be to eliminate personality. If I make every decision in imitation of someone else, personality disappears. I seldom find it helpful, therefore, to make decisions by asking myself what Jesus would do in a given situation.

Personal preference is a good guide to righteous action to

the extent that it has been molded and shaped by God's values and principles. If we truly embrace God's worldview, our preferences will reflect that commitment. Recognizing our sinfulness, we must check our preferences to make sure that they are neither immoral nor unwise. But once we have done that, we are free to follow our preferred course of action.

Agreement and Disagreement

You can find Christians defending different and sometimes opposite positions on any social and political issue. Should this be? In an ideal world, would all Christians agree on what should be done in a particular situation?

The discussion above makes it clear that Christians could disagree at several points in their assessment of righteous action. The first check on our actions eliminates inherently evil acts. Because the concept of what is inherently evil is generated directly and solely from God's worldview, there should be no disagreement on this. If two people disagree as to what is inherently evil, at least one is wrong.

When it comes to deciding whether an act is unwise, though, disagreement is not surprising. In many instances it is difficult to determine if an action is unwise. But because this, too, is rooted in God's worldview, there should be a correct answer. If two Christians disagree about whether a given action is unwise, at least one is wrong. So, again, in a perfect world Christians would not disagree as to what is unwise.

Christians, however, might very well prefer different emphases or approaches to the same problem. Ideally their goals would be the same and their approaches compatible, but they need not decide to take the exact same action. For instance, one person may stress the role of government in solving the problem, while another stresses the role of private individuals. One may take an aggressive, activist approach, while another takes a quiet, low-key approach. These differences are controlled, at least in part, by personality. As long as we are not acting evilly or unwisely, we are free to allow our personality to determine action.

It is important to recognize that not all differences of opinion between Christians are differences of right and wrong. Of course, some are, and those need to be addressed humbly at the level of theology. But others are not. We must be tolerant and even appreciative of those various manifestations of righteousness. Every Christian has a part to play in God's plan for the world, and each part is different. As we each pursue righteousness, God will bring about His purposes.

CLARIFYING OUR THEOLOGY

KNOWING HOW GOD thinks about an issue, as opposed to what God thinks *we* should do in a particular situation, is primarily a matter of thinking through our theology more carefully in a particular matter. As I explained earlier, our theology is a model of God's worldview based on the Bible and experience of reality. As we receive new information, we incorporate it into our theology and thus slowly expand it. When the urgency of making a particular decision points to a deficiency in our theology, we are forced to rethink our information and see if we can improve our theology to allow us to make our decision. The process we go through to do this is essentially the same that we use to construct our theology in the first place, with one difference: the impetus for constructing our theology is a desire for additional information; the impetus for rethinking our information is the need to make a pressing decision. Nevertheless, because they appear to be different processes, I will demonstrate how one clarifies a theology. By its very nature, such a demonstration is somewhat artificial and simplistic. I do not want to give the impression that the process is simple or cut-and-dried. What follows is more of an illustration than a fully developed argument.

Speaking of Spotted Owls . . .

For many years a battle has raged in the Pacific Northwest over the spotted owl. Environmentalists have been lobbying hard for the preservation of large areas of habitat. Loggers have been arguing that the government has gone too far in an effort to protect this particular species. At issue is the survival of one species of bird; without protection it might become extinct. Would this be wrong? Let us go to work on this question: "Would it be wrong for man to do anything that might cause the spotted owl to become extinct?" We need to break this question down into more manageable ones and then examine each one carefully while constantly referring back to the Bible and experience for any necessary information.

1. Is the preservation of an individual creature's physical life the most important thing there is? If the answer to this question is yes, then we are done. If God considers the preservation of an individual creature's physical life the most important thing there is, then nothing should override that consideration, and we should place the same importance on it. Clearly, however, other things are more important to God than the preservation of physical lives. God allows plants, animals, and even humans to die every day even though He could prevent their deaths. Therefore, God must consider something more important than physical life. On the other hand, just because God allows things to die does not mean that we can. Because God is God, He enjoys certain privileges that we, being humans, do not share. Should we humans do all we can to preserve life? Obviously not. In many instances God commanded men to take the lives of animals in sacrificial ceremonies. Also, God told man he could eat meat. Therefore, there are some things more important than preserving the life of an individual creature.

In the specific situation involving the spotted owl, we are not talking about just any old animal; we are talking about one of the last surviving members of a species. If these spotted owls die without offspring, the species will no longer exist on the earth. Does this fact make this situation more significant than a situation involving an individual animal? Could God want every species to be preserved? We will tackle this question with two more questions:

2. Does God care about the preservation of species? There is good evidence that God is concerned about the preservation of species. Recall the story of Noah. God asked Noah to build a large ark whose purpose was to provide a way for Noah, his family, and animals to escape death from the Flood. The animals God wanted to protect were not just Noah's house dog, Fido, and the kids' pet hamster, Guido; God saved pairs of all the animals so that those species would continue to survive and multiply. (Having gone to all the work to create the species in the first place, He does not want to have to keep reinventing the eel.)

3. Why did God preserve the species? God could have wiped out all of creation in the Flood and started over. But He did not. Why didn't He? Surely it was not any easier for Him to save a remnant of creation than to start all over. He must have had another reason. God has shown a great deal of commitment to the redemption of man and the creation over which man is to rule. He could have destroyed it all as soon as Adam and Eve sinned (that would have been very reasonable), but from that moment until now, God has followed another course of action: God has been committed to the salvation of man and the restoration of creation. His actions during the time of Noah were in keeping with this commitment; His preservation of the animals during the Flood reflects His desire that mankind, to whom God has given dominion over the animals, also be saved. It appears, therefore, that God preserved the species to demonstrate His determination to save and restore all of creation.

4. Should man take care to preserve the species? Man and creation are closely tied together. Because creation has been entrusted into man's care, clearly the well-being of creation is an indicator of man's performance. What remains to be investigated is whether man must guarantee the continuing existence of all species in order to be a good manager of creation. Let us look at the two possibilities.

It could be that the preservation of all the species indicates man's faithfulness as a manager of God's creation. In this view, to allow a species to die out necessarily entails negligence on man's part. If man is a good manager of the earth's resources, he will not allow a species to die out; if a species does die out, then man has been a bad manager of the earth's resources. So, in this view, preserving the species would be a part of man's job description, much like fidelity is part of a husband's job description. For a husband to be unfaithful to his wife is to fail at his job— *adulterer* and *responsible husband* are mutually exclusive terms. Likewise, according to this view, man cannot commit species genocide and be a good manager of the earth's resources at the same time.

The other possibility is that, while man is to be a good steward of the earth's resources, in the course of carrying out his responsibilities he may irrevocably eliminate a species from the face of the earth. Being a good manager of the earth's resources could very well mean taking steps that would result in the elimination of a species.

In this view, man's responsibilities would be like those of a good citizen. It is a true statement that a good citizen obeys the laws, but is it true by definition or by generalization? Could a good citizen break a law and still be a good citizen? Recently I was driving down the street, minding my own business, when I came to a red light. I stopped. I waited. And I waited. I waited for about fifteen minutes. Cars backed up behind me for two blocks. Having the quick mind that I do, I surmised that the light was stuck. I remembered from my driver's manual that red means stop, green means go, and yellow means Mack trucks can go but Hondas would be prudent to stop. If I were to go through the red light, I would be breaking the law. Being a good citizen, I do not want to break the law. But the purpose of the law is to create a well-ordered society, and traffic lights help to do this, except in a few large metropolitan areas. This light, however, was causing disorder; traffic was being impeded, not facilitated. So I cautiously went through the intersection. Was I being a good citizen? I think so. The job of a good citizen is to do his part to make sure society conducts itself in a fair and orderly manner. In this case that goal was best accomplished by breaking the law.

It is entirely possible that man's job of overseeing creation is like being a good citizen. In general, he will preserve the resources God has provided. But man's job is not just to make sure everything is retained; he is to use these resources wisely for his purposes. His actions, therefore, could cause a species to become extinct, yet he would incur no condemnation from God. As stated earlier, however, preserving the species could be a part of man's job description. Therefore, allowing a species to die out would be to fail at his job. How do we decide between these two options? We have to go back and rummage around in our memory banks to see if we can figure out which option best fits what we know about God. We will decide between these two options by answering another question:

5. *Is it always wrong for man to cause a species to become extinct?* Because I cannot think of any passages in Scripture that would resolve this question, let us turn to another resource: experience. Some species in this world (viruses, for example) cause incredible human pain and suffering. Man has spent untold dollars and hours trying to eliminate certain particularly harmful viruses, such as polio. Is there any reason to think that man is being irresponsible in trying to eliminate these species from the face of the earth? I think not. Perhaps viruses fit into a separate category from more-advanced species. Are there any more-complex organisms that clearly need to be exterminated? I do not know much about such things, but let us use gypsy moths as an example. Wherever these moths with voracious

appetites go, they destroy large numbers of trees; a scorched-earth policy is the only tactic they know. This moth is unwanted in all fifty states. If it were gone forever, would it be missed? Again, I think not. Perhaps its absence would have harmful repercussions for the ecological balance of nature, but I seriously doubt that any imbalance would outweigh the advantage of being rid of this insect. Dealing with the consequences of exterminating the moth would become part of man's job. It is a never-ending job. As long as creation is under God's curse because of man's sin, creation will frustrate man's efforts to manage it. So then, experience seems to indicate that in the process of managing the earth's resources it might sometimes be necessary for man to take steps that result in the extermination of a species of living creatures.

On the basis of our discussion, it seems to me that God is not interested in us preserving every species of animal just so that we have them. Man's assignment is broader: God wants him to use the earth's resources wisely. Although some of these resources may be used up or eliminated in the process, this is not automatically wrong. Man's job is like that of a farmer who owns a piece of land. The farmer could see his job as that of museum curator and therefore retain everything just as it was when he bought it; he can try to get as much out of the land as quickly as he can and then sell it, or he can work the land with the goal of leaving it in better condition than when he got it (which may mean getting rid of some resources, such as rocks, swamps, and old rusted car bodies). I am suggesting that man is like the farmer whose goal is not to make sure that the piece of land retains everything but instead to make the land even more useful for farming. Likewise, every generation of men should leave the earth in better condition than it was before they were born so that the conditions of living become steadily better with each generation. Whatever man does toward this end without violating other divine principles is justified.

What, Then, Do We Conclude?

Is God opposed to the spotted owl's becoming extinct? Not necessarily. There is nothing automatically wrong with man taking action that endangers the continued existence of the spotted owl. Therefore, should protections of the spotted owl habitat be removed? Not necessarily. We must resolve another issue first: what constitutes wise management of the earth? Just because taking actions to cause the extinction of a species is not necessarily wrong does not mean such actions should therefore be taken. The question is what use of the spotted owl habitat is best from a comprehensive and long-term perspective. Before we, as Christians, could responsibly take a position for or against the preservation of spotted owl habitat, we would have to resolve this question in a manner similar to what we just discussed.

Regardless of what we think about the spotted owl, we would do well to use the process I just described to arrive at a conclusion that reflects God's thinking. It is simply a matter of taking what we know about God and His handiwork and using that knowledge to clarify our theology with respect to the issue at hand. The task requires careful, methodical thought. When we are finished, however, our theology is more complete. In the future, when we have decision-making questions, this more complete theology will be better able to answer any related questions raised. By continually asking decision-making questions and clarifying our theology in those areas where it is inadequate to enable us to make our decisions, we slowly improve our theology until it eventually comes to approximate God's worldview.

SOME CAUTIONS

AFTER WE HAVE carefully built our theologies, we must still take care. Even if we have a good theology, we can apply it poorly. If we are not careful, our desires and personal prejudices can overrule our theology. When I was growing up, I was taught that smoking is wrong—so wrong, in fact, that a person who smokes must not be a Christian. I no longer believe this is true. I am convinced there is nothing inherently immoral about smoking. (I still think it is a dirty, disgusting habit, but then so is auto racing.) When I discover that someone smokes, however, my first response is to think that person must not be a Christian. This response does not come from my theology (it is not even consistent with my theology); it is just a habit I developed in my childhood that continues to this day. I have to force myself to view a smoker through my theology and not through my prejudice. This takes effort, but if I am to look at the world as it really is, I must look at it from God's perspective, not through my own prejudices.

A second thing we need to keep in mind as we try to apply biblical principles in our lives is the fact that some issues become more complicated than we might initially think due to the cultural significance of certain actions. We must understand not only God's worldview, but we must also thoroughly understand our own culture. Another example may help clarify the reason for this.

Let us say I am overcome with an irresistible desire to wear a baseball cap backward. As far as I know, there is no reason to think that the direction of a cap bill, in and of itself, has any moral import. In our day, however, clothes and fashion have become important social and political statements. As I understand it, our high schools are divided into myriad subcultures, each with its own set of values and cultural norms. One who is knowledgeable about such things can tell just by the way a student is dressed to which subculture the student belongs. Therefore, because clothes can be much more significant than just something to cover the body, I need to ask additional questions: What would I be saying if I were to wear a baseball cap backward? And do I want to say that?

Because our culture is changing so quickly, fashions that begin with strong social or political associations can become part of the popular culture and lose their original significance within a few years, if not months. I suspect that wearing a baseball cap backward fits into this trend. When people first started doing it, it probably had a strong association with gangs. But having become so common, it has lost that association. Now, as far as I know, wearing a baseball cap backward has no meaning at all.

Whether or not you agree with my analysis, I hope you can see that it is important for us to be students of our culture. We need to know how to read actions in the context of our society so that we can accurately interpret the actions of others and so that we can accurately represent our beliefs to others.

APPLYING JAMES 5:14-15

HOW SHOULD WE apply our sample passage, James 5:14-15? This is a little tricky because, as I hope I have already made clear, we do not apply isolated verses or passages; we apply a full theology. A well-constructed theology is built on passages—in fact, on all the passages—of the Bible. Therefore, we cannot apply James 5:14-15 alone, but we can apply a theology built in part on James 5:14-15.

The contribution James 5:14-15 made to our theology came in the form of principles. Let us look at those principles once again:

1. God comes to the aid of the repentant.
2. One who wants help in his struggle against his faithlessness is repentant of that faithlessness.
3. Faithlessness is ultimately a reluctance or refusal to accept what is true.
4. The best antidote for faithlessness is a clear understanding of God's perspective on things.
5. Wise believers have the best understanding of God's perspective on things.

6. God likes to use people as instruments of His ministry.
7. Physical symbols (such as the oil) can help people understand what is happening spiritually.

Let me describe an all-too-frequent scenario to show how we could put these principles into effect in our lives. A young man, Pete, whom I knew in high school, goes away to college. When I visit him after six months of college life, he is a changed person. As a high school student, Pete was a committed believer. Every indication was that he truly trusted Jesus as Lord and Savior. He was considerate, calm, and respectful. The minute I see him at college, however, I notice he is different: he looks different, dresses stylishly and extravagantly; his temperament is more surly and sarcastic; his room is decorated with cheesecake photography and his windowsill is decorated with empty beer cans. In short, Pete shows signs of having been seduced by the university culture.

Pete tells me about his college experience and intimates a little of the difficulty he has had in adjusting. In the course of our conversation, he mentions George. George is a mature believer and a mutual friend. Pete's words regarding George are guarded, but a certain amount of respect and fondness is detectable.

With James 5:14-15 in mind, I ask Pete if he would like me to arrange a meeting between him and George to discuss the difficulties he has had in acclimating to university life. Pete says he would like to talk to George. So I arrange for George to meet with Pete and me. When I talk to George, I inform him of the situation and tell him that it looks to me like Pete has lost sight of what it true and is knuckling under to the pressures of his peers. I also tell George that, as I read the situation, Pete is still willing to be persuaded of the reality of God and Christianity.

When the three of us meet, we begin with a briefing on what each has been doing for the last few months. Later, George gently raises the issue of the state of Pete's faith. Pete shows an eagerness to continue in this line of discussion, so we forge ahead. George and I listen to the questions with which Pete has been wrestling for the past few months and respond to them as best we can. Pete denounces his past belief in God as naïve and questions the uniqueness of Christianity, claiming that all religions are basically the same. We do not deny that his past belief was naïve; we only point out that that does not make it wrong—it just needs to mature. As to the uniqueness of Christianity, George argues that this indicates an inadequate understanding of Christianity. Christianity is indeed unique, and if its claims are true, it precludes the other religions of the world. George went on to restate the gospel as an explanation of the claims of Christianity.

I would say that this scenario illustrates a sound application of the principles derived from James 5:12-14. There are some obvious similarities between this situation and the situation James described, but there are also some notable differences. Pete, the one struggling with faithlessness, did not call anyone; I called in help. The pressures facing Pete are much different from those facing James' audience. No elders were called; no oil was used; no prayer was prayed. Despite all of these differences, some of the principles I derived from James 5:12-14 informed my choice of actions. I applied my theology.

CONCLUSION

IN THESE LAST two chapters I have attempted to explain how one moves from interpretation to application. I can probably best summarize the process with a diagram:

→ THEOLOGY →	
Three Steps to Developing a Theology	**Three Questions for Testing a Decision**
1. Gather Information.	1. Is it wrong?
2. Interpret information.	2. Is it unwise?
3. Determine principles.	3. Am I fooling myself?

Two different things are happening. On the one hand (the left side of the chart), we take information from experience and the Bible, interpret it, draw principles from that interpretation, and then weave those principles into a model of God's worldview, which I have called a *theology.* On the other hand (the right side of the chart), we apply that theology to situations as they arise. We determine our preferred course of action, and then we submit it to three tests to see if it is righteous. The first test eliminates any inherently evil course of action. If it passes that test, the second test checks to see if the costs outweigh the benefits. The third test examines motives. If a course of action passes all these tests, then it is righteous.

The process I have described is the well-established way we all bridge the interpretation–application gap in everyday situations, and it is only reasonable that God would expect us to use this same process with respect to revelation. Because it is particularly difficult, however, and because so much is riding on our conclusions, we need to discipline ourselves to use this process carefully and deliberately as we process the biblical texts. Only then can we build a sound theology.

Why didn't God provide us with a more foolproof method of determining what He wants us to do in any given situation? He could have. He could have issued each of us a Urim and Thummim—tools used by ancient Israelite priests for determining God's will—to consult when we have a question. But God did not do it that way.

Every difficult decision requires us to sort through our understanding of what God values and what is true. And every serious review of our understanding leads to further and further clarification. Rather than just doing what we are told, we come to see the world through God's eyes.

Furthermore, as we wrestle with difficult decisions, it is often hard to keep straight in our own minds what is true and what we would like to be true. The rebellion in us runs so deep that we are constantly tinkering with the evidence. We are always trying to stack the deck in such a way as to justify what we want. This tendency is so strong that we do it without even being aware of it. Consequently, with every decision we must search our souls to make sure that we want to be obedient and are not lying to ourselves. Ultimately we cannot know what is in our hearts, and we are at the mercy of God to reveal to us our own rebellion. Every big decision is a time for us to reexamine our hearts and ask anew whether we want our will or God's will to be done.

If God had wanted more than anything else for us to always take the right action, He should have given us each a Urim and Thummim. But if His emphasis is on helping us to understand and embrace His worldview from the bottom of our hearts, the way He has chosen is best.

STUDY QUESTIONS

1. What biblical principles come to bear on the issue of abortion?

2. Acts 15 provides a description of the council in Jerusalem. At that meeting the apostles debated whether it was necessary for Gentile believers to be circumcised. List the biblical principles that Peter and James brought to bear on this issue.

3. In Galatians 2:3 Paul wrote, "Not even Titus, who was with me, though he was a Greek, was compelled to be circumcised." And yet in Acts 16:3 we read, "Paul . . . took [Timothy] and circumcised him because of the Jews who were in those parts."

   a. What were the principles behind Paul's action in Galatians 2:3? In Acts 16:3?

b. Build these principles into a coherent worldview that can help you answer the question "When do we submit to the religious scruples of others, and when do we not?"

CHAPTER EIGHT

A Single Level of Meaning

Alice looked on with great interest as the King took an enormous memorandum-book out of his pocket, and began writing. A sudden thought struck her, and she took hold of the end of the pencil, which came some way over his shoulder, and began writing for him.

The poor King looked puzzled and unhappy, and struggled with the pencil for some time without saying anything; but Alice was too strong for him, and at last he panted out, "My dear! I really *must* get a thinner pencil. I can't manage this one a bit; it writes all manner of things that I don't intend—"

IN CHAPTER TWO DAVID Crabtree articulated our conviction that the Bible communicates on one and only one level, namely, the level of its human author's intent. As he argued there, seeing the Bible as communicating through ordinary language is the most reasonable perspective one can take. Furthermore, it is an important, inescapable fact that in ordinary language we tacitly presume there to be one and only one level of meaning (that which the author intended) and we seek *that* meaning—nothing more, nothing less.

Even if someone could construct a statement that could be construed to say two distinct, equally valid things, unless the author had explicitly instructed us so, we could never know that both meanings were intended. The statement's irresolvable ambiguity would paralyze us with indecision. We would feel compelled to choose between the two different interpretations, but we would be unable to find a basis for choosing one over the other. It would fail to communicate *any* meaning to us, for we would have no way to decide which meaning is the right one. In ordinary language the simultaneous communication of two distinctly different meanings is impossible.

Whether the Bible communicates on multiple levels is highly controversial. For most of the history of biblical interpretation, various Bible interpreters have advocated multiple levels of meaning. An exhaustive defense of our theory of a single meaning would require an involved discussion of many complex, technical issues—well beyond the scope of this work. We must settle for a more modest goal: to explain and illustrate our position clearly, hoping that it will prove compelling to the reader's common sense.

Early in my study of the Bible, I believed the Bible communicated at multiple levels, at least in certain portions of the book. My attention had been drawn to the way the New Testament authors used the Old Testament. It seemed apparent that these authors were seeing meanings in Old Testament texts that were not derived from their ordinary level of meaning. So where were they finding them? How were they seeing what I could not see?

Were they making up fanciful, fallacious interpretations with no basis in fact? That was too unsettling even to consider. These men were articulating the gospel for all future generations. Their understanding was based, in part, on their reading of the Old Testament. If their reading of the Old Testament was bogus, if their interpretations were fanciful nonsense resulting from absurd and invalid exegesis, then the faith they espoused was a joke or, even worse, a fraud. It had no integrity. That could not be right; there had to be an alternative.

The only alternative—it seemed—was that these New Testament authors were seeing meanings that were truly there. I could not see them, but they could. Presumably, these apostles understood God's purposes, methods, and intent better than I. Accordingly, they could see higher levels of meaning than I could. What they saw was really there, though not in the surface meaning of the text. It was in a higher level of meaning, and I was not trained in the methods and modes of reasoning required to discover such a higher level of meaning. Therefore, in order to discover all the meaning God had encoded in the Bible, I would have to learn from the New Testament authors the methods whereby those extraordinary levels of meaning could be discovered.

I set that task for myself—to understand how the New Testament authors interpreted and reasoned about the Old. Assuming there were multiple levels of meaning in the text— and operating on that assumption—I began to develop what I thought was a reasonable, commonsensical theory of biblical interpretation that could rationally permit multiple levels of meaning. But that was early in my experience. The more experience I gained (that is, the more I understood the apostles' message and their reasoning from the Old Testament), the less I saw any evidence that they were appealing to some higher level of meaning. Eventually, I arrived at the point where I knew of no clear instance of an apostle appealing to an extraordinary level of meaning.

My studies followed a typical pattern. While an apostle's use of the Old Testament would appear—on a superficial reading—to depend on some extraordinary level of meaning, upon closer examination, I saw that it did not. A better, more accurate understanding revealed that the New Testament author was reasoning from the ordinary level of the text's meaning after all. I concluded that there was no justification for a theory of biblical interpretation that espouses multiple levels. The New Testament authors offered no support for such a theory, and if they offered no support, then no reason remains to advance such a theory. My only reason for advocating multiple levels of meaning had evaporated on me and I was forced to return to the commonsensical position being espoused in this work: in the Bible, God has communicated His message through ordinary verbal communication, and in ordinary verbal communication there is one and only one level to its meaning. A language statement means what its author intends it to mean—nothing more and nothing less.

My purpose in this chapter is to examine one representative example of an apostle's citation of the Old Testament. My hope is that it will dramatically illustrate what has been my repeated experience. I observe a use of the Old Testament that looks, at first blush, like an appeal to some higher level of meaning; then, on closer examination, I come to see that it is nothing of the sort.

To better appreciate the following discussion, the reader would do well to read and reflect on Matthew 1:18-25 and Isaiah 7.

THE TRADITIONAL UNDERSTANDING OF MATTHEW 1:22-23

MATTHEW 1:22-23 SEEMS straightforward to the typical modern reader. Matthew was claiming that Jesus' birth to the young virgin Mary was the very event that God had straightforwardly predicted through His prophet Isaiah: "Behold, the virgin shall be with child and shall bear a Son, and they shall call His name Immanuel." This reading of Matthew 1:22-23 is entrenched in our cultural understanding. Centuries of Christmas sermons, Christmas pageants, and Christmas carols have instilled it in all of us. Jesus just *is* Immanuel, the predicted son of a virgin. Everyone knows that; nothing could be clearer.

There is, however, a problem with this traditional interpretation, one that our cultural tradition has largely ignored. Isaiah predicted that a virgin would bear a son whose name would be Immanuel. Matthew's claim, according to the traditional interpretation, was that Isaiah was predicting the birth of a son

named Jesus. If the name of Mary's son is not the name predicted by Isaiah, how can we maintain that Jesus is the son
whose birth Isaiah was predicting? An obvious response would
be that Isaiah was not predicting that Immanuel would be the
son's name; rather, he was predicting a title or description that
would aptly describe this son. That is reasonable enough. But
the angel who appeared to Joseph in a dream was predicting—
even dictating—the *name* to be given to Jesus when he said,
"You shall call His name Jesus, for He will save His people from
their sins" (Matthew 1:21). If "you shall call His name Jesus"
means "you shall give Him the name Jesus," then it seems
equally likely that "they shall call His name Immanuel" means
"they shall give him the name Immanuel." If this is so, then
there is a discrepancy between the prediction and the alleged
fulfillment. This discrepancy may be a clue that the traditional
interpretation has not accurately grasped what Matthew understood to be the relationship between Isaiah's prediction and
Jesus' birth.

HISTORICAL BACKGROUND

IF WE IGNORE what Matthew said about Isaiah 7, what is the
most straightforward understanding of what Isaiah was predicting there? We must explore that question, beginning with
an understanding of its historical background.

In the mid-730s B.C., King Pekah of Ephraim and King Rezin
of Aram joined forces against Judah.[1] Previously, Pekah and
Rezin had requested an alliance with Ahaz, the king of Judah.
Because Assyria was a growing threat in the region, Pekah and
Rezin wanted Judah to join them in an alliance for mutual
defense against Assyria. Ahaz refused to join. Consequently,
Pekah and Rezin decided they had to defeat Judah, depose
Ahaz, and replace him with a puppet monarch who would
cooperate with them.

When Ahaz learned that these joint forces had mustered

for battle, he and all the people of Judah were overcome with fear. In the midst of their terror God delivered a message to Judah and Ahaz through the prophet Isaiah:

> Take care and be calm, have no fear and do not be
> fainthearted because of these two stubs of smoldering
> firebrands, on account of the fierce anger of Rezin
> and Aram and the son of Remaliah (Pekah). . . . [Their
> plan to depose you] shall not stand nor shall it come
> to pass. . . . If you will not believe, you surely shall
> not be established. (Isaiah 7:4-9, adapted)[2]

A short time later, Isaiah delivered another message to Ahaz regarding the same issue: "Ask a sign for yourself from the LORD your God; make it deep as Sheol or high as heaven" (Isaiah 7:11).

In reply, Ahaz told Isaiah, "I will not ask, nor will I test Yahweh (the Lord)!" (verse 12, adapted). To this, Isaiah responded:

> Listen now, O house of David! Is it too slight a thing
> for you to try the patience of men, that you will try
> the patience of my God as well? Therefore, the Lord
> Himself will give you a sign: Behold, a virgin will be
> with child and bear a son, and she will call His
> name Immanuel. He will eat curds and honey at the
> time He knows enough to refuse evil and choose
> good. Now before the boy will know enough to
> refuse evil and choose good, the land whose two
> kings you dread will be forsaken. Yet Yahweh will
> bring on you, on your people, and on your father's
> house such days as have never come since the day
> that Ephraim separated from Judah; he will bring on
> you the king of Assyria. (Isaiah 7:10-17, adapted)

Isaiah's prophecy went on to predict a total devastation of the land of Judah. The armies of the Assyrians, Isaiah predicted, would overrun Judah and spoil the land completely (see Isaiah 7:18-25).

How, exactly, are we to understand these predictions and the events surrounding them? The most straightforward way to understand what Isaiah was saying to the people of Judah goes something like this:

> Do not fear Pekah and Rezin. True, they have mustered their troops against you, but their plot to defeat you and overthrow Ahaz will not succeed. Indeed, not only will they not harm you but in addition they themselves will be destroyed soon. A young woman is about to have a son; she will name him Immanuel. Before this Immanuel is old enough to know right from wrong, Ephraim and Aram will be forsaken.
>
> But while you need not fear Pekah and Rezin, there is something else you should fear. Not immediately, but in the not-too-distant future (at a time when the boy Immanuel knows enough to refuse evil and choose good [Isaiah 7:15]), the land of Judah will be overrun by the Assyrians and be completely laid waste.

Isaiah described the coming devastation in terms of being reduced to eating "curds and honey" (Isaiah 7:15,22). In the context of the prediction taken as a whole, the eating of curds and honey was clearly meant to describe the result of a tragic event. Most likely it indicates the destruction of the domestic agriculture of the land so that the people would be reduced to foraging off the wild, uncultivated land for survival. This is what Judah could expect from the Assyrians in the not-too-distant future.

Events transpired just as Isaiah had predicted. Within a

short span of time, Assyria invaded Aram and Ephraim, con-
quered them, took the people into exile, and destroyed them
politically. About thirty years later, Assyria came against Judah
with the intent of laying siege to Jerusalem. But hearing a
rumor that the king of Cush was coming up against them, they
left to oppose him instead. Though they vowed to return, God
saw to it—through a series of events—that they never
returned to lay siege to Jerusalem. Just as Isaiah had predicted,
while Judah was completely devastated, Jerusalem remained
unconquered and at peace (for the time being).

THE MEANING OF ISAIAH'S MESSAGES

THE HISTORICAL BACKGROUND to Isaiah's prophecies is
relatively clear. But what, exactly, is the content of Isaiah's
messages to Ahaz? How are we to understand their particu-
lars? Isaiah 7 consists of two separate messages to Ahaz and
Judah. At first glance, it may appear that Yahweh's first message of comfort to Judah (Isaiah 7:3-9) was simply that they
did not need to fear defeat at the hands of Pekah and Rezin.
Such a reading is quite plausible, but on closer inspection we
will see a somewhat different comfort being offered. And in
any event, the second message (Isaiah 7:10-17) clearly offers
a different comfort. We must consider the meaning of these
messages more closely.

Isaiah's First Message

To understand Isaiah's first message, note that it ends like this:
"If you will not believe, you surely shall not be established"
(Isaiah 7:9, adapted). What, exactly, were the people of Judah
to believe in order to "be established"? And what does it mean
to "be established"?

Isaiah 7:9 is reminiscent of the famous statement from
Habakkuk that Paul (Romans 1:17; Galatians 3:11) and the
author of Hebrews (Hebrews 10:37-38) cited as evidence that

we are justified by faith rather than by works of the Law.

> Record the vision
> And inscribe it on tablets,
> That the one who reads it may run.
> For the vision is yet for the appointed time;
> It hastens toward the goal, and it will not fail.
> Though it tarries, wait for it;
> For it will certainly come, it will not delay.
> Behold, if anyone shrinks back [from believing it],
> My soul has no pleasure in him;
> But the one who is righteous will live by virtue of
> his believing it.
> (Habakkuk 2:2-4, adapted)

Isaiah 7:9 and Habakkuk 2:4 have this in common: there was a sort of person who would "be established" and a sort of person who would not. The one who would be established (or who, in the language of Habakkuk, "will live") was he who believed the hopeful message that God had delivered. The one who did not believe would not be established.

What is this hopeful message that these two prophets were claiming the righteous man would believe? In citing Habakkuk, Paul revealed what he understood this hopeful message to be: it was the "vision" that Habakkuk was to inscribe on tablets, and it ultimately amounted to nothing less than the overarching vision of what God had destined for His people Israel.

Throughout the Israelites' history, God continually reminded them of a promise He had made to Abraham: the day would come when a generation of Abraham's descendants would form an entire nation of people who would faithfully love and serve Yahweh. Such was the overarching vision of their destiny. It was the promise that ought to have defined their identity as a people.

The challenge before Israel was to persist in believing that this promise would be realized. As days, years, decades, and centuries passed without that nation being established, believing that it would ever come to pass became more and more difficult. And believing became an even more acute problem when they encountered circumstances that threatened to make its realization impossible. To be specific, if an enemy came against Israel, it was more than a threat to the comfort and well-being of that present generation; it was a threat to their very identity as a people. If their enemy succeeded, robbing them of their Promised Land and taking away their autonomy as a people, how would God's promise to them ever be fulfilled? Their possession of the land and their political autonomy were prerequisites to its fulfillment, and defeat by an enemy would destroy these preconditions. And if this enemy wiped out the whole lineage of Abraham in the process, the fulfillment of God's promise would be rendered impossible.

Throughout their history there were presumably two kinds of people in Israel. First, there were those who believed in, identified with, and personally placed their hope in the distant, unseen fulfillment of this defining promise that God had made to Abraham. Second, there were those who did not believe the promise, instead concerning themselves with nothing more than their own personal peace and prosperity. In the time of Ahaz, what mattered to this latter sort of Israelite was that Rezin and Pekah be prevented from invading their land, destroying their vineyards, tearing down their houses, and raping their wives. That is what *they* feared. But the other sort of Israelite (if any existed) had a different sort of fear. His fear was that the success of Rezin and Pekah would mean that God had forsaken Israel and that He was no longer intent on keeping His promise. To the one who believed God's grand, overarching promise, Isaiah's message of comfort would go something like this:

> Your vineyards are about to be destroyed, your
> houses torn down, your children killed, raped, or

taken captive. But have no fear! God has not forsaken you. He has not forgotten the promise He made to Abraham. He will eventually return your descendants to your promised homeland. He will establish them there and turn their hearts to Him so that they will faithfully serve Him. And they will prosper under His care just as He promised long ago.

This message offered no comfort whatsoever to the unbeliever—to the one whose only desire was for personal comfort and safety. Such a person would see no value in a guarantee that in some distant, future generation God's promise to Abraham would be realized. It was to just such an unbeliever that the prophet Isaiah said, "If you will not believe, you surely shall not be established" (Isaiah 7:9, adapted). Likewise, it was to just such an unbeliever that Habakkuk said, "If anyone shrinks back [from believing the promise made to Abraham and the vision of Israel's future implicit in it], my soul has no pleasure in him" (Habakkuk 2:4, adapted). Both prophets were offering the same message to the people of Israel: the person who was pleasing to God and who would, as a consequence, be blessed by God in the age to come was the one who took an interest in what God had promised and who delighted in the purposes of God being realized in history. The person who would enter into life in the age to come was the one who believed that God would do what He had said He would do and who embraced those divine purposes as good and valuable. The person who disregarded what God had said He would do, considering God's purposes to be irrelevant and uninteresting, would not enter into life; that is, he would not enter into blessing in the age to come.

This, I maintain, is the message that Isaiah was delivering to Judah in 7:4-9. He was not saying, "Do not be fainthearted because of these two stubs of smoldering firebrands, Pekah and Rezin. Do not fear that they will disrupt your personal peace and prosperity, for their plot will not succeed." Rather, he was saying, "Do not be fainthearted because of these two. Do not fear that they will destroy the possibility of God's promises to Abraham ever being fulfilled. Their silly plot will come to nothing. Believe Me and rejoice in this guarantee! For if you do not, you do not stand to inherit God's blessing in the age to come." The fact that the prophets repeatedly delivered just such a message makes it all the more likely that this is what Isaiah meant in 7:4-9.

Isaiah's Second Message

Even if I am wrong about Isaiah 7:4-9, the meaning I propose for it is certainly very similar to the comfort offered by God's second message to Ahaz (Isaiah 7:10-17). Yahweh told Ahaz that he would be given a "sign." A sign of what? A sign that Judah's peace and prosperity would not be disturbed? Certainly not! Isaiah's second message had two aspects: First, a child was about to be born, and *before* that child would be old enough to know right from wrong, Aram and Ephraim (the two kingdoms Ahaz feared) would be destroyed. Second, a child was about to be born, and sometime *after* that child would be old enough to know right from wrong, Assyria would overrun Judah and devastate it. The "promise" that their personal peace and prosperity was going to be destroyed was an essential part of Isaiah's message, so the accompanying sign could hardly be a guarantee that their peace and prosperity would not be disturbed.

"God with us." A clue to the meaning of this sign is contained in the child's name. Immanuel means "God with us." God was promising to be "with" Israel. But with them to do what? Not to protect them from material and physical devastation. Rather, God was with them in order to protect and preserve them so that His promises regarding Abraham's children would not be jeopardized. This is the only interpretation of the sign that makes any sense when we take into consideration the entire context of Isaiah's prediction. And as we saw above, it

is all the more likely in light of the frequent repetition of this assurance to Israel.

Most of Judah never appreciated the value of this reassurance. They had no real regard for the fulfillment of God's purposes. But to a small remnant, it would have been received as a wonderful message of hope: "Have no fear. Although your vineyards may be torn down, your houses leveled, your families taken into captivity, and you yourselves killed, God's promise still stands. He has not forsaken His people. His purposes will come to pass. Glory be to God." That is the message symbolized in the child's name, Immanuel—"God with us."

Immanuel's identity and conception. Two questions still remain: (1) Who was this child, Immanuel? (2) Was Isaiah describing a supernatural conception, the birth of a child to a virgin?

In all likelihood Immanuel was a natural-born child of Isaiah's wife. We see a distinct pattern in the early portion of Isaiah: God had a message for Israel; He had Isaiah and his wife conceive a child; He instructed Isaiah what to name the child. The name was intended to encapsulate in slogan form the message God had for Israel. That child then lived in the midst of the people as a living billboard, reminding them of the prophetic word given to Isaiah.

It appears that one such living billboard had already been born to Isaiah's wife. The name of Isaiah's son Shear-jashub, which means "a remnant will return," has all the earmarks of being a prophetic word to Israel, sloganized in a child's name (Isaiah 7:3).

In chapter 8 we find another such slogan-child:

> Yahweh said to me, "Take for yourself a large tablet
> and write on it in ordinary letters: Swift is the booty,
> speedy is the prey. And I will take to Myself faithful
> witnesses for testimony, Uriah the priest and
> Zechariah the son of Jeberechiah." So I approached

the prophetess [presumably, Isaiah's wife], and she
conceived and gave birth to a son. Then Yahweh
said to me, "Name him Maher-shalal-hash-baz
[which translated means "swift is the booty, speedy
is the prey"]; for before the boy knows how to cry
out 'My father' or 'My mother,' the wealth of Damascus and the spoil of Samaria will be carried away
before the king of Assyria." (Isaiah 8:1-4, adapted)

Notice that the same feature exists in this prophecy that we
find in the prophecy regarding Immanuel in chapter 7. God
tied the timing of his prediction to the approximate age of the
child—"before the boy knows how to cry out 'My father' or
'My mother' . . . " This is similar to "before the boy knows
enough to refuse evil and choose good . . . " and also to a similar statement in Isaiah 7:15-16.

So we have a pattern. Before Immanuel's birth was predicted, Isaiah had a son to whom a message-name was given.
After Immanuel was born, Isaiah had a son to whom a message-
name was given. Immanuel was intended as a "sign" to Judah
by virtue of the message encapsulated in his name. If we had
no knowledge of Matthew's linking Immanuel to a virgin birth,
we would most certainly conclude that Immanuel, like the
message-children before and after him, was a message-child
born to Isaiah and his wife.

Objections to Immanuel's nonvirgin birth. Two objections
could be raised to such a conclusion: (1) Doesn't the fact that
Isaiah described it as a "sign" require that it be some sort of
miraculous birth—a virgin birth, for example? (2) Because
Isaiah 7:14 specifically predicts that a "virgin" would be with
child, how could Isaiah be the father and his wife the mother?

The Hebrew word translated "sign" in Isaiah 7:14 is at times
used to refer to miraculous events (for example, Exodus 10:2;
Numbers 14:22; Deuteronomy 4:34; 6:22; 11:3), but that is not
its primary meaning. Primarily, the word denotes a symbol or

token. Isaiah predominantly used it to describe a token that had been given to symbolize a specific message or meaning (see, for example, Exodus 13:9,16; 31:13,17; Deuteronomy 6:8; Isaiah 19:20; 20:3; 37:30; 55:13). Isaiah 8:18 reads:

> Behold, I and the children whom the LORD has given me [presumably Maher-shalal-hash-baz, "swift is the booty, speedy is the prey" (Isaiah 8:1-4); Shear-jashub, "a remnant shall return" (Isaiah 7:3); and Immanuel, "God with us" (Isaiah 7:14)] are for signs and wonders in Israel from the LORD of hosts, who dwells on Mount Zion.

The Hebrew word translated "wonder" *(mopheth)* is primarily used to denote a symbol or sign, especially a token of some future event. In this passage, then, Isaiah explicitly announced the fact that his children were living symbols of God-given messages to Israel. That is the sense in which they were "signs." They were not signs because there was anything miraculous about their circumstances or births. They were signs because their God-given, inspired names were enduring prophetic messages. Nothing about the way Isaiah used the term *sign* requires it to denote a supernatural miracle of any sort. Hence, it does not require a virgin birth of Immanuel.

But did not Isaiah explicitly state that Immanuel would be born of a virgin? Not necessarily. The meaning of the Hebrew word translated "virgin" is somewhat controversial. According to many Hebrew scholars, it does not primarily denote a woman who lacks sexual experience. Instead, it denotes a female at a particular stage of life—one arriving at early womanhood.

Consider a young woman being described as a "teenage mother" in our society today. In contemporary American culture a teenage woman is typically unmarried. Hence, *teenage mother* carries with it a presumption that she is an unmarried mother. But her marriage status is only secondarily suggested; it is not the primary meaning of the phrase. The phrase *teenage mother* could just denote a married teenager who has borne a child.

The Hebrew term *'almah* ("virgin") in Isaiah is analogous to this. *'Almah* denotes a young woman just arriving at early womanhood. In ancient Hebrew culture, women of that age, while marriageable, were typically not yet married. Hence, they were typically without sexual experience—virgins. But to describe a woman as an *'almah* did not specify that she was a virgin; it merely specified that she had just arrived at early womanhood. *'Almah* could, therefore, denote a recently married female who had borne a child. That would be atypical, perhaps, but it would be possible.

If Isaiah had wanted to highlight explicitly the fact that the mother of Immanuel was to be a virgin, *bethulah* is likely the word he would have used. According to Hebrew scholars, *bethulah* more definitively suggests the woman's lack of sexual experience than does *'almah*. As we have already seen, the most straightforward way to understand Isaiah 7 is that Isaiah's wife was the *'almah* who would conceive and bear Immanuel. And in all likelihood Isaiah's wife was a mother already, for Isaiah already had a son (Isaiah 7:3). If that is right, then clearly she was not a virgin, and *'almah* was not being used to indicate that she was.

The timing of Immanuel's birth. One more piece of evidence supports the conclusion that Isaiah's wife was the mother of Immanuel. Unless my reasoning from Isaiah 7 is mistaken, Immanuel was to be born within a short time of the prediction of his birth, not several centuries later. Here is my reasoning:

Part of Isaiah's prediction was that "He [Immanuel] will eat curds and honey at the time He knows enough to refuse evil and choose good" (Isaiah 7:15). As we saw above, this is a prediction of the total devastation of Judah—a devastation that would occur sometime after Immanuel was old enough to know right from wrong. If we arbitrarily set that age at six, then Isaiah was saying that around the time Immanuel was six years old Judah's complete devastation would take place. But at the same time, Isaiah's prediction required that this devastation had to occur within the life span of Immanuel because the prediction said Immanuel himself would forage for curds and honey in a decimated Judah. If we arbitrarily set Immanuel's life span at seventy years, then Judah's devastation had to occur within seventy years of Immanuel's birth. To summarize, Isaiah's prediction explicitly specified that the devastation of Judah would occur somewhere between six and seventy years after the birth of Immanuel.

So it is clear when Judah's devastation had to occur relative to the birth of Immanuel. But at what point in history would Immanuel be born? Wouldn't Isaiah's prediction allow for Jesus—born around the turn of the first century A.D.—to be Immanuel? If Judah's predicted devastation were to occur sometime between the birth and death of Jesus, then why not? As required by Isaiah's prediction, Ephraim and Aram would have been destroyed *before* such a first-century Immanuel knew right from wrong—about seven centuries before. It would appear that a first-century Immanuel would meet the requirements imposed by the letter of the prediction:

> "He will eat curds and honey at the time He knows enough to refuse evil and choose good. For *before* the boy will know enough to refuse evil and choose good, the land whose two kings you dread will be forsaken." (Isaiah 7:15-16, emphasis added)

But there are two problems with identifying Immanuel as Jesus. First, the only "devastation" of Judah in the first century A.D. occurred in A.D. 70, when the Romans brutally put down a Jewish revolt. If Jesus was Immanuel, then He did not "eat curds and honey" as a result of this devastation in

A.D. 70, for He had died, been raised, and ascended into the heavens some forty years before this devastation. The facts of the first century and Jesus' life do not fit the scenario described in Isaiah's prediction.

The second problem is that the identification of Immanuel as Jesus does not conform with what Isaiah most likely intended. According to the most natural reading, Isaiah was attempting to locate two events relatively close in time. To be specific, he was trying to locate the destruction of Aram and Ephraim and the devastation of Judah within the lifetime of one person. Between the time that Immanuel was born and the time that he was old enough to tell right from wrong, Ephraim and Aram would be destroyed. But then within this same Immanuel's lifetime—specifically, *after* he reached the age of moral discernment and *before* his death—Assyria would decimate Judah. This is the most straightforward way to understand what Isaiah was saying. Otherwise, it is difficult to see how Immanuel could serve as a sign to Ahaz (Isaiah 7:14). How, for example, could the child Jesus be described as a "sign" given to Ahaz—as a reminder of God's promise that He would be "with" Judah—when Jesus was nowhere to be seen in the lifetime of Ahaz? So while the letter of Isaiah's prediction, with regard to the timing of Judah's devastation, could conceivably be fulfilled by Jesus, that is not the best way to understand what Isaiah intended. On its most natural reading, Isaiah's message to Judah was this: "You don't have to worry about Pekah and Rezin. They will be out of the picture shortly—before Immanuel can tell right from wrong. However, you *do* have to worry about the Assyrians. Within this Immanuel's lifetime, you will be overrun by them." Understood this way, a first-century Immanuel—Jesus—would not do. It had to be an Immanuel who was born shortly after the prediction.

Furthermore, history itself dictates that we locate the birth of Immanuel in the same time period as this prediction. Historians have established the destruction of Ephraim and Aram at around 732 B.C. The Assyrians' devastation of Judah most likely took place around 700 B.C. Using these dates, in order for the destruction of Aram and Ephraim to have occurred before Immanuel was old enough to know right from wrong and in order for Immanuel to have personally experienced the devastation of Judah, Immanuel's birth would have had to occur sometime before 735 B.C. That would make Immanuel somewhat over thirty years old when the Assyrians overran the land of Judah—just as Isaiah had predicted.

DID MATTHEW KNOW WHAT HE WAS DOING?

WHEN WE COMPARE how Matthew appears to have understood Isaiah 7 to a straightforward, reasonable interpretation of Isaiah 7, we have a dilemma. Under its most likely interpretation, Isaiah 7 is predicting the birth of a child sometime in the eighth century B.C. Matthew seems to have been suggesting that Isaiah was predicting the birth of the baby Jesus in the first century A.D. This is a significant discrepancy. What are we to make of it?

Some interpreters deny that Isaiah was predicting a contemporary Immanuel and maintain that instead he was making a simple, straightforward prediction of the birth of Jesus. I cannot agree. In light of the reasoning outlined above, it seems inescapable to me that Isaiah meant to predict the birth of a child within his own lifetime. So the denial of an eighth-century Immanuel cannot be the solution to our dilemma.

But there are still two other proposed solutions worth investigating—and in the end, rejecting.

Inspired Falsehood?
Some scholars take the position that Matthew—by construing it as a prediction of Jesus' birth—was offering a fallacious interpretation of Isaiah 7. Although his interpretation of Isaiah 7

was wrong, Matthew offered us something true and inspired nonetheless. That is, while he made a mistake in interpretation, his mistake was a divinely inspired mistake that led to his espousing an inspired truth, namely, that Jesus is the Messiah who, in an important sense, is Immanuel, "God with us." From this view, it is of no consequence that Matthew's understanding of Isaiah 7 was based on invalid exegesis involving wrongheaded reasoning leading to a fallacious understanding of the scriptural text. What is important is that Matthew got the truth about Jesus right.

This solution to our dilemma is unacceptable. The integrity of the gospel itself is on the line. Whether Matthew's mistaken exegesis was fraudulent and self-aware or innocent and unintentional, he offered us Isaiah 7 as support for his claims about Jesus and the gospel. If what he offered us as authoritative support for that teaching is nothing but bogus, nonsensical, invalid, illegitimate exegesis, how can we—with intellectual integrity—accept Matthew's teaching?

Appealing to Matthew's being an inspired apostle does not help. Inspired falsehood is still falsehood. And it makes no sense to me that God's revealed *truth* could be founded on a whole network of falsehoods. If I go on believing that Matthew spoke the truth about Jesus when I know that one of the acknowledged bases for what he claimed is manifestly false, how am I not being intellectually irresponsible? Am I not desperately holding on to something I know to be false and choosing to believe that it is true anyway?

Some people call such an attitude "faith." For them, faith is the moral and spiritual virtue of being able to believe something to be true when you know that any reasonable person would judge it to be false. But this is contrary to a truly biblical conception of faith. Biblical faith is not an alternative way of knowing and believing something—a way to believe when you cannot believe on the basis of reason and evidence. Rather, biblical faith is nothing more and nothing less than a moral and spiritual openness to accepting any and every truth that reason and the evidence indicate to be true. The believer is the person who bows to the truth even when he sees (from the evidence and sound reason) that it will require him to bow his knee to God. The unbeliever is the one who—when he sees that the evidence and sound reason must lead him to acknowledge God—is quite willing to forsake the evidence and sound reason rather than bow his knee to God.

Given the nature of the faith God is requiring of us, we are to embrace and believe what the evidence and sound reason recommend to us. But the theory of "inspired and truthful falsehood" suggests something contrary to this: (1) God inspired the apostles to engage in fallacious exegesis of Scripture. They drew conclusions that were true even though those conclusions were not warranted by the scriptural texts from which they were drawn. (2) God, through the apostles, offered up this fallacious interpretation of Old Testament Scripture as part of the basis upon which we are to be persuaded of the truth of the gospel. (3) Then God called upon us to accept and embrace this gospel as true. If this were in fact what God has done, it would be a violation of everything God requires of us. God, in calling us to such a faith as this, would be calling us to forsake intellectual responsibility. That cannot be right. Quite to the contrary, in calling us to faith God is calling us to an intellectual integrity and responsibility that does not come naturally to people who are in rebellion against God, reason, and truth. For this reason, I cannot accept the position that Matthew was offering a true understanding of Jesus based on a false understanding of Isaiah's prediction in Isaiah 7. This is not an acceptable solution to our dilemma.

Double Prediction?

Other Bible students seek to solve the dilemma by maintaining that Isaiah 7 must involve a double prediction. Taken in its ordinary sense, it predicts an eighth-century-B.C. Immanuel,

242 | The Language of God

but at some higher level of meaning—above and beyond the ordinary sense of the text—it simultaneously predicts the birth of Jesus.

This would solve our dilemma, if it were possible. But how is it possible? As we have maintained above (see pages 221-222), even if God could compose a text that could validly be construed to predict two distinct events simultaneously, how could we ever know—without instruction from God—that both predictions were intended? Both predictions could never be successfully communicated. We could guess, speculate, wonder, suspect, wish, hope that both predictions were intended to be conveyed by the prophet's language. But how could we ever know?

Such a perspective requires Matthew to be suggesting something like this:

> Now Isaiah is predicting a child, Immanuel, to be
> born in the time of King Ahaz. But I want you to trust
> me on this. He is also at the same time predicting the
> birth of Jesus to the virgin Mary 730 years later. I
> know it doesn't look like it. The ordinary meaning of
> Isaiah's prediction merely predicts a son in the time of
> Ahaz. But God intended us to understand Isaiah's
> prediction on a whole different level as well. At that
> other level, God is predicting the birth of Jesus. I
> know you can't see it, but trust me—it's there.

I cannot accept this. It is problematic to think that Matthew would appeal to Isaiah 7 as support for and illumination of who he understood Jesus to be at the same time that he believed that the relevance of Isaiah 7 to Jesus was invisible to all but the inspired apostles. Matthew clearly expected his readers to be able to see the relevance of Isaiah 7 to the issue of Jesus' identity. But if so, then he must have believed that he was appealing to a reasonable, accessible, and ordinary level in Isaiah's meaning, not to an esoteric, higher level of meaning that only he and other inspired apostles could see.

For reasons already discussed, it is not acceptable to postulate an extraordinary level of meaning to anything in the biblical text, not even to a prophetic prediction. So we are left with our dilemma: how are we to respond to Matthew's apparent reading of Isaiah as a prediction of the birth of Jesus when it is quite clear that that is not what Isaiah intended?

RETHINKING MATTHEW'S CLAIM

THE SOLUTION TO our dilemma rests in realizing that—contrary to the traditional understanding—Matthew was not viewing Isaiah 7 as a prediction of the birth of Jesus. In order to see this, we must come to a fresh understanding of what the apostles meant when they said that an event "fulfilled" a prophetic prediction.

Fulfillment of Scripture

When a New Testament writer told us that some event X "fulfilled" what a prophet had said, we immediately assume we know what he meant, namely, that event X was the event predicted by the prophet. No other option even crosses our mind. But as a matter of fact, the New Testament authors had a much broader, more inclusive understanding of what it meant for an event or set of circumstances to fulfill the Old Testament Scriptures.

Learning how the New Testament writers use the term *pleroō*—the Greek term that is typically translated "fulfill"—is an important step toward seeing this. Notice the use of *pleroō* in James 2:21-23:

> Was not Abraham our father justified by works when he offered up Isaac his son on the altar? You see that faith was working with his works, and as a result of

> the works, faith was perfected; and the Scripture
> was fulfilled [pleroō] which says, "And Abraham
> believed God, and it was reckoned to him as right-
> eousness," and he was called the friend of God.

Two things are of note about this statement: (1) The text that James quoted (Genesis 15:6) is *not* a prediction; it is a state-ment of fact. It describes a truth about Abraham at a particu-lar point in his life. Namely, Abraham responded to a particular promise God had made to him by believing it, and by virtue of that belief God counted Abraham as justified. Hence, what-ever James was saying, he could not have been saying that Genesis 15:6 predicted Abraham's offering up of Isaac on the altar, for this earlier passage is not a prediction at all. (2) The citation—"And Abraham believed God"—makes no direct and explicit reference to Abraham's sacrifice of Isaac. Rather, it refers to Abraham's accepting God's promise to be true: he would be the father of a vast number of descendants. It refers to nothing more and nothing less. This raises an important question: on what basis did James link such a statement to the sacrifice of Isaac?

When we understand the overall argument of the second chapter of James, it becomes clear what James was arguing. Genesis 15:6 tells us that God considered Abraham justified on the grounds that Abraham believed the promise God had made to him. But on what basis can we know that Abraham did, in truth, believe God's promise? Not simply on the basis of Abraham's saying so. We know that he believed the promise and trusted the God who had made it when we see Abraham's willingness to obey God even to the point of sacrificing Isaac. Seemingly, killing Isaac would destroy any possibility of Abra-ham becoming the father of a vast set of descendants. That is, it would destroy the possibility of God's promise being ful-filled. Hence, if Abraham had not believed that God was trust-worthy and His promise sure, he could never have willingly sacrificed his son. Because he was willing, it is evident that he *did* believe that God's promise was sure. That is James' point: if a person believes God's promises, that will be evident by his actions (by his "works").

We have already noted that the assertion "Abraham believed God, and it was reckoned to him as righteousness" (James 2:23, quoting Genesis 15:6) is not a prediction. In what sense, then, was Abraham's willingness to sacrifice Isaac a fulfillment of it? In this specific sense: the reality of Abraham's believing God's promise was, in a way, brought to completion by Abraham's willingness to act in harmony with such a belief. If Abraham had been unwilling to sacrifice Isaac, it would mean that his belief in the promise of God had never reached a point of settled conviction. His actions would have betrayed the fact that he did not really trust God to keep His promise after all. But because his belief made itself manifest in actions arising from and consistent with that belief, his belief proved itself real, authentic, complete, and wholehearted. In James' language, Abraham's belief was "made full" *(pleroō)* by his action.

James' use of *pleroō* is instructive. In it we find a New Testament writer claiming that a Scripture was fulfilled when he clearly could not have meant that some event X was the very event predicted by that Scripture. This runs counter to the common view that an event "fulfills" a scriptural text if that event is predicted by the text. But James' use of *fulfill (pleroō)* makes it clear that that is not how the New Testament writers employed the term. In fact, when a New Testament writer said, "And the Scriptures were fulfilled which say . . . ," there is a wide range of possibilities for what he saw as the relationship between the New Testament event he was seeking to explain and the text of the Old Testament that he cited. What all is included in that wide range of possibilities? That can be determined only by an inductive study of all the places where the New Testament writers used the formula "And the Scriptures were fulfilled." What is important for our purposes is this: when we encounter this formula, it does not automatically mean that a prophetic prediction has come to pass. On the contrary, the New Testament writers used it in a variety of ways.

God with Israel in Christ

So what does *pleroō* mean in Matthew 1:22? We have already discussed what Isaiah 7:14 likely meant in its original context. When Isaiah said, "Behold, a virgin will be with child . . . , and she will call His name Immanuel," Isaiah was describing a son who was soon to be born to his wife and who would be given a name that was God's message to contemporary Judah. What was that message? "God will be with you." And what did that mean? That God would remain faithfully on the side of Judah, the chosen people of God. That He had not forsaken them. Whatever might happen in the short term—whatever hardship, suffering, and defeat they might experience—the promise of God would be kept. Some coming generation of the children of Abraham would be made secure in the Promised Land and would be given a heart to love and follow God. God's promise would not fail, no matter how unlikely that might seem in the light of their present circumstances.

What would be required in order for God's overarching promise to the seed of Abraham finally to be realized? According to the teaching of the New Testament, the Messiah and the forgiveness for sins that He would bring were necessary preconditions for God's keeping the "new covenant" that He promised to keep with the house of Judah and the house of Israel (see Jeremiah 31:31-34). The forgiveness of sins is not only a precondition for individual salvation; it is a prerequisite for God's fulfillment of each of His promises to Abraham. In order to establish a society of Abraham's descendants whose sins would be forgiven, whose hearts would be circumcised, and who would walk faithfully in God's ways, God had to supply a true High Priest who could mediate between the sinful people of God and the holy God Himself, appealing to God for mercy on their behalf. According to apostolic teaching, Jesus is that High Priest. Without Him, there could be no fulfillment of any of the promises God made to Abraham.

Immanuel was a sign to Judah, a living billboard declaring that God would indeed faithfully fulfill the promise He had made to Abraham. But if, as Matthew understood, there could be no fulfillment of that promise without the coming of the appointed High Priest, then the time when that High Priest finally entered into history was a significant and remarkable step toward the fulfillment of God's promise to Abraham. Indeed, it was the crucial, indispensable, central event. The High Priest having come, God's promise would ultimately be fulfilled. This is the perspective that informs Matthew's comment. In the birth of Jesus—the one sent by God to be the true High Priest—one finally sees a reality come into being that will culminate in God's promise to Abraham being realized. Seven centuries earlier, Matthew was saying, God set up a billboard in the midst of Judah (namely, the child Immanuel), reminding Israel that God would fulfill His promise to Abraham no matter what the Assyrians might do. Now, Matthew said, we see a reality set in place—the birth of the true High Priest—that portends the fulfillment of that same promise, the fulfillment of that which Immanuel symbolized.

This, I believe, is what Matthew meant when he said that the birth of Jesus took place "to fulfill what was spoken by the Lord through the prophet" (Matthew 1:22). What Immanuel was in name only—the promise that God would eventually fulfill His promise to Abraham—Jesus was in substance and reality. The coming of Jesus into the world was itself a promise that God was at work finally to fulfill the promise He had made to Abraham hundreds of years before. Jesus was Immanuel not because He was the son whom Isaiah predicted but because His very existence meant—far more dramatically and emphatically than the name of Isaiah's son ever could—that the promise of God would certainly come to fruition. Immanuel meant "God is with Israel" in name only; Jesus meant "God is with Israel" in reality. The birth of Jesus was the concrete action of God to begin to fulfill what He had promised Abraham.

CONCLUSION

WE HAVE EXAMINED only one instance of the New Testament citing the Old. That is barely a start. To understand truly how the apostles understood the relationship between the gospel and the Old Testament Scriptures, one would have to study each citation in its own right. There are different nuances to each and every claim that "the Scriptures were fulfilled." But the passage we have looked at above is, in important respects, representative of every New Testament use of the Old. It is therefore instructive.

So long as we assume that the formula "the Scriptures were fulfilled" describes an event that the New Testament author believed to have been predicted by the Old Testament, we are at risk of forming a distorted and inaccurate understanding of how the New Testament authors viewed the Old Testament. In my earliest studies of the New Testament, I harbored an unspoken fear that the writers of the New Testament were simple-minded, naïve exegetes who were content to base their understanding of Jesus and the gospel on invalid, forced, or even absurd interpretations of the Old Testament text. After years of study and reflection, I have changed my mind. I have come to see that the authors of the New Testament were intelligent, insightful, rational, sophisticated, knowledgeable, careful, commonsensical, and accurate interpreters of the Old Testament. Not only were they careful and accurate interpreters of the grammar and syntax of each individual statement, but more importantly, they had an accurate and profound grasp of the Scriptures' message as a whole. Earlier, when I was embarrassed by how naïve and unintelligent their use of the Scripture seemed, it was my interpretation that was flawed, not theirs. While their interpretations of Scripture were, in truth, reasonable and insightful, my interpretation of them had been in error!

Several years of study later, I have become confident that an exhaustive study of every use of the Old Testament by a New Testament author would lead to these conclusions:

1. The New Testament authors assumed a single level of meaning to the text of the Old Testament.
2. They understood that single level of meaning to consist in what the relevant author intended the text to communicate.
3. The interpretive methods they employed were nothing more and nothing less than the commonsensical principles of interpretation familiar to us all.

In short, the New Testament authors believed the Scriptures to be God's Word to us in the form of normal verbal communication. There is nothing spooky or supernatural about the way the Bible communicates. It is unique and remarkable in its content, not in its form. It is supernatural in *what* it says, not in *how* it says it.

STUDY QUESTIONS

1. Consider 1 Corinthians 9:9-10 in context. Was Paul saying that the commandment in the Law—"You shall not muzzle the ox while he is threshing"—is *not* a commandment to not muzzle an ox while he is threshing and is actually intended by God to require something else?

2. Study Matthew 2:13-15. There Matthew explicitly claimed that Jesus' exile in Egypt to escape the murderous plot of Herod was a "fulfillment" of a statement in Hosea 11:1, "Out of Egypt I called My Son." Study the entire message of Hosea 11 and try to understand the statement "Out

of Egypt I called My Son" in its context there.

    a. Is Hosea 11:1 a prediction?

    b. Did Matthew understand Hosea 11:1 to be a prediction of Jesus' exile in Egypt?

    c. If the facts of history had been different—if, instead of fleeing to Egypt, Jesus' family had fled to Macedonia—could Matthew have composed the following with equal validity: "So Joseph got up and took the Child and His mother while it was still night, and left for Macedonia. He remained there until the death of Herod. This was to fulfill what had been spoken by the Lord through the prophet: 'Out of Egypt I called My Son'"?

    d. Finally, what was Matthew's line of reasoning? To what purpose did he cite Hosea 11:1 in Matthew 2:15? What does Hosea 11:1 contribute to what Matthew wanted to say to the readers of his Gospel?

  3. Take a look at Matthew 2:16-18. Matthew 2:18 claims that the weeping of the mothers of Bethlehem "fulfilled" what was said in a passage out of Jeremiah. Study Jeremiah 31:15 and its context.

    a. Is Jeremiah 31:15 a prediction? If so, of what is it a prediction? If not, what is it and what does it mean?

    b. Did Matthew understand Jeremiah 31:15 to be a prediction of the mourning of Bethlehem's mothers?

    c. Finally, what was Matthew's line of reasoning? To what purpose did Matthew cite Jeremiah 31:15?

In what sense was Herod's murder of the innocent babies in Bethlehem a fulfillment of Jeremiah
31:15? (Hint: Consider whether Revelation 12:4
might suggest something that would link Jeremiah
31:15 and Matthew 2:16-18 together.)

4. Study Matthew 2:19-23. The statement "He shall be
called a Nazarene" cannot be found anywhere in the whole
of Old Testament Scripture.

a. How could Matthew attribute to the prophets a
statement that none of them ever made?

b. Was Matthew attributing these words to the Old
Testament prophets? Or was he rather attributing
the meaning and sentiment contained in these
words to the Old Testament prophets? If the latter,
what meaning or sentiment do they convey?

c. Finally, what was Matthew trying to say when he
claimed that Jesus' birth in Nazareth was the fulfillment of a statement that was never actually
made in the Old Testament?

Taking the Bible Seriously

THE AUTHORS OF THIS book have argued for a specific approach to understanding the Bible. We have labeled it the commonsense approach, but we could also describe it as the ordinary language approach. What we have been arguing, in effect, is this: to arrive at an accurate understanding of the Bible, we must understand that it communicates through ordinary human language, and we must interpret it accordingly. We must use common sense and our knowledge of the dynamics of ordinary language to interpret it. If we ignore common sense and treat the Bible as something other than ordinary human language, then we will fail to reach an accurate understanding of the intention of the biblical authors.

Why have we dealt with these matters at such length? What is at stake? It is our conviction that all who take the Bible seriously must be willing to re-evaluate the methods they use in interpreting it. All who want to know the truths revealed in the Bible ought to be willing to read it in the way God intended. The issues addressed by this book are vitally important, because our very access to the truths of God is at stake. If the authors of this book are right, then anything other than the ordinary language approach will lead to misunderstanding and error. Anyone who takes the

Bible seriously must be willing to confront these issues.

To conclude our discussion, I want to (1) discuss why we must take the Bible seriously and (2) outline the responses we hope to have encouraged in you through our discussions in this book.

IS IT NECESSARY TO TAKE THE BIBLE SERIOUSLY?

EVERYTHING I HAVE said so far assumes the importance of taking the Bible seriously. But who says so? What difference does it make whether we arrive at an accurate understanding of the actual intention of the biblical authors? Isn't that the preoccupation of spiritually impoverished academics? If we truly love Jesus, what difference does it make how accurately we understand the Bible? The Christian faith is not about getting it right; it is about loving Jesus! These sentiments reflect a prevalent, but diabolically inaccurate, understanding of what the Christian faith is all about.

In the preceding chapter we saw what Isaiah taught: the person who will inherit eternal life can be distinguished from the person who will be condemned by whether he believes the truth revealed by God. If to "have faith" is to understand, to consider, to like, and to embrace the truth of who God is and what He has purposed in cosmic history, then he who has faith will stand; he who does not have faith will fall. This perspective is not unique to Isaiah—it is the consistent teaching of the whole Bible.

As we saw in the preceding chapter, this is not to say that we are saved by "getting it right." The Bible does not teach justification by sound doctrine; it teaches justification by a sound heart. We will be saved if our heart longs to know God and His truth, if our heart is responsive to truth rather than hostile toward it. But a heart that is responsive to truth will accept it when confronted with it. And the heart that is not responsive to truth will reject it when confronted with it. That is why Isaiah could say, "If you will not believe, you surely shall not be established" (Isaiah 7:9, adapted). Isaiah was saying, "If you will not believe, you will not be saved."

But that brings us back to our initial question. If the basis upon which the Bible connects belief and salvation is the responsiveness of the person's heart, doesn't that make actual knowledge of the truth superfluous? If I have a heart that is open and responsive to truth, what difference does it make whether I actually come to know what the Bible teaches? Isn't a heart that is open to its truth sufficient? Am I required to come to an accurate understanding of what the biblical authors intended to teach?

To answer that, we must inquire further regarding the character of the heart that is receptive to truth. How would such a heart respond when thwarted in its search for truth? Would it accept defeat, saying, "Oh well! The Bible is too hard. I will never understand it. But that's okay; I'll get eternal life anyway"? The receptive heart could never respond so. Jesus taught that the heir of eternal life will "hunger and thirst for righteousness" (Matthew 5:6). By the same token, the heir of eternal life will hunger and thirst after truth. This is implicit throughout the biblical message. The heir of life will not be dissuaded in his search for truth. He will not be daunted by the difficulty of the quest. He will and must persist. The truth is nourishment and satisfaction to his soul; he will not be denied.

In the time of Isaiah, God made an explicit promise to the people of Judah that confronted them with an important truth. Their response, Isaiah told them, would test the character and condition of their hearts. Today, between the covers of our Bibles, we have the entire truth of who God is, what He has promised, and what He purposes to accomplish in cosmic history. Yet the Bible's meaning is not transparent. Therein lies the test for us. How we respond to the difficulty of interpreting the Bible reveals the character and condition of our hearts.

If I am content with "Oh well. The Bible's too hard for me. I can't understand it," and if I close the book, walk away from it, and never give it another thought, then I will not inherit eternal life. Such a response reflects the same damnable condition of heart that, in the time of Isaiah, refused to believe his message. But if I am undaunted by the obscurity of the Bible, persisting in my quest to understand it through whatever means and resources I can find, then certainly I am an heir of life, for such is the person who will "be established."

The person who takes the Bible seriously—wanting to understand what it is saying in order that he might believe its message, place hope in its promises, and live his life in the light of its truth—is one who will have life in the age to come. The person who does not take the Bible seriously has no part in the eternal kingdom. Regard for the Bible is not just one of a number of ways to love God, not one legitimate option among many. The consistent message of the biblical authors leads to an inescapable conclusion: how we regard the truth revealed in the Bible is a decisive sign of whether we will inherit eternal life. Because (as the apostle Paul insisted) justification comes to those who believe, one's failure to take the Bible seriously is a clear indication that he does not believe and has not been justified.

What we do with the Bible is a life-and-death issue! It is not enough to "love Jesus" while remaining indifferent to the message of the Bible. How we respond to the Bible is all of a piece with how we respond to Jesus.

DESIRED RESPONSES

IN CONCLUSION, HERE are seven important responses we earnestly hope that you, the reader, will have to our book. This book has been a success if you do any of the following:

1. Understand the difference between a plausible interpretation and the right interpretation. For those who view doctrinal debate as a contest and not a shared quest for revealed truth, it is sufficient to show that a given text *could* mean such-and-such. They view the possibility that a text could be construed in a particular way as a license to do so. But the goal of biblical interpretation is not to find supporting evidence for one's current understanding of doctrine; it is to find what the biblical authors intended. To settle for a plausible interpretation of a passage that supports one's doctrinal preconceptions is to misuse the Bible. To rightly use the Bible, we must discover what the biblical authors actually did intend. The important thing is not what a text *could* say; the important thing is what it *does* say!

2. Think critically about claims regarding the meaning of the Bible. Many different claims are made about the message of the Bible. Our hope is that our discussion of biblical interpretation has put you in a better position to think critically about all such claims. There are many ways to misinterpret the biblical text; there is only one way to get it right. That fact should motivate us to be critical of what others claim on behalf of the Bible.

3. Study the Bible for yourself. Our many traditions have put the Bible in a cage. My fellow authors and I hope that we have set it free—in your mind—to speak for itself. Having realized that there are fresh insights to be gained, may you be reenergized to seek them out. The Bible is not a mere rubber stamp of tradition; it is a fresh and vital message that puts every tradition to the test. Accordingly, it is well worth studying to find out what we have yet to learn.

4. Reexamine your theological tradition. Our loyalty must be first and foremost to the message of the Bible, not to a particular theological tradition. No theological tradition is completely wrong, but neither is any infallible. All should be respected and heard, but all stand in need of correction. Our ongoing task as disciples of Jesus is to listen anew—to study afresh the message of the Bible and to permit it to stand in judgment over us and our ideas.

258 | The Language of God

5. Interpret the Bible according to the same principles you would use to interpret any other written work. You may be well trained in the reading and interpretation· of difficult literature, such as the literature of philosophy, fiction, poetry, math, or science. You should feel free to employ the interpretive skills you have already acquired in your study of the Bible. The Bible is not, in principle, different from any other text with respect to how it conveys its meaning.

6. Develop your skill at biblical interpretation. It would be a mistake to think that reading this book can equip you to do the task of biblical interpretation. We have presented a theory of biblical interpretation, but to *do* biblical interpretation, personal skill is needed. Biblical interpretation is an art, and art is effectively accomplished only by developing one's skill at that art through practice.

7. Live your life in the light of the gospel. This is the most important response of all. Speaking for David, Ron, and myself, I can assure you that our interest in biblical interpretation is not merely academic. There is no value in understanding the message of the Bible if you do not embrace its message as true and live your life on the basis of that truth. First and foremost, therefore, this book is an exhortation for you to seek out the truth in order that you might live your life in its light.

May God reveal Himself to you more each day as you faithfully interpret His book using the common sense He gave you.

Notes

CHAPTER TWO: The Goal of Interpretation

1. This quotation is from an earlier version of the New American Standard Bible.

2. Fyodor Dostoyevsky, *The Diary of a Writer,* trans. Boris Brasol (Santa Barbara, CA: Perigrine Smith, 1979), p. 28.

CHAPTER THREE: Language Conventions

1. Berkeley and Alvera Mickelsen, "Does Male Dominance Tarnish Our Translations?" *Christianity Today,* October 5, 1979, p. 23.

2. Wayne Grudem, "Does *Kephale* ['Head'] Mean 'Source' or 'Authority Over' in Greek Literature? A Survey of 2,336 Examples," *Trinity Journal* 6NS (1985), p. 46.

3. An example of how to use an exhaustive concordance appears in the first study question at the end of this chapter.

CHAPTER FOUR: Context and Coherence

1. In the mid-1970s I took a class on biblical interpretation from J. A. Crabtree that changed my life. The following exercises, all of which require that we consider verses in their original contexts, are from that class.

Chapter Five: Background Information

1. E. D. Hirsch, *Cultural Literacy* (Boston: Houghton Mifflin, 1987).

2. I. Epstein, ed., *The Babylonian Talmud: Seder Nashim,* trans. H. Freedman (London: Soncino, 1936), Nedarim·30a.

Chapter Six: Building a Biblical Worldview

1. Please go to www.mckenziestudycenter.org/bible/language

Chapter Eight: A Single Level of Meaning

1. Ephraim and Judah were the two kingdoms formed when Israel split in two after the time of Solomon, Ephraim being the northern kingdom and Judah being the southern kingdom. Aram was an ancient kingdom located roughly where Syria is today.

2. Here and in other such places where the word *adapted* is used like this it indicates that the biblical quotation is my own translation adapted from the New American Standard Bible.

About the Authors

DAVID CRABTREE

DAVID HAS BEEN a teacher at McKenzie Study Center in Eugene, Oregon, since 1981. He is also president of Gutenberg College, which he helped found, and one of the pastors of a Eugene church called Reformation Fellowship. In his teaching at McKenzie Study Center, David has focused on doctrine, biblical languages, Genesis, church history, and philosophy of education. Currently, he is most interested in studying the impact of modernization on the way people see the world.

David has a B.A. in Russian language and literature from the University of Washington, an M.A. in classical Greek from the University of Oregon, and a Ph.D. in history from the University of Oregon. He has studied and lived in St. Petersburg (formerly Leningrad), Paris, and Rome. He and his wife, Susan, currently live on a small farm just outside of Eugene, where they raise and home-school their four children.

J. A. CRABTREE

JOHN A. ("JACK") Crabtree, brother of David, has been a teacher at McKenzie Study Center since 1981. He is also a teacher at Gutenberg College, a pastor of Reformation Fellowship, a regular participant on two weekly radio shows (*In Search of Truth* and *Christianity at Work*), the author of several papers, and a contributor to three previous books. While

Jack has wide interests and a broad background, over the years he has focused primarily on arriving at a clear understanding of biblical Christianity and coming to an accurate understanding of biblical hermeneutics.

Jack has a B.A. in philosophy from Stanford University and a Ph.D. in philosophy from the University of Oregon. Before coming to McKenzie Study Center, he served as a pastor and teacher in a biblical studies program at Peninsula Bible Church in Palo Alto, California. Jack and his wife, Jody, have four surviving children—a married daughter who teaches elementary school, a son and a daughter in college, and a daughter in high school. They currently live in Eugene, Oregon.

RON JULIAN

RON HAS BEEN a teacher at McKenzie Study Center since 1981. Ron is also a teacher at Gutenberg College, a pastor of Reformation Fellowship, a regular participant on a weekly radio program *(In Search of Truth)*, and the author of *Righteous Sinners*, published by NavPress. During his years at the study center, Ron's focus has been on doing biblical exegesis and communicating the gospel. In addition to biblical studies, his interests include film, music, literature, and computer technology.

Ron has a B.A. in linguistics from the University of Oregon. Before coming to McKenzie Study Center, he served as a teacher in a biblical studies program at Peninsula Bible Church in Palo Alto, California, where he taught Greek and Hebrew. Ron and his wife, Robby, live in Eugene, Oregon, with their two children, Brian and Erin.